Neda Guderzi
Narges Pourshahi Aghchekand

Analysis of Criminalization Violations of Intellectual Property

Neda Guderzi
Narges Pourshahi Aghchekand

Analysis of Criminalization Violations of Intellectual Property

Based on Imamiyyah Jurisprudence Teachings

Noor Publishing

Imprint

Cover image: www.ingimage.com

Publisher:
Noor Publishing
is a trademark of
Dodo Books Indian Ocean Ltd. and OmniScriptum S.R.L publishing group

120 High Road, East Finchley, London, N2 9ED, United Kingdom
Str. Armeneasca 28/1, office 1, Chisinau MD-2012, Republic of Moldova, Europe
Printed at: see last page
ISBN: 978-620-5-63425-7

Analysis of Criminalization Violations of Intellectual Property Based on Imamiyyah Jurisprudence Teachings

By

Neda Guderzi

Master's Degree in Criminal Law and Criminology, Islamshahr Islamic Azad University, Islamshahr, Iran

Narges Pourshahi Aghchekand

Master's Degree in Criminal Justice and Criminology, Non-Profit Institution of Rushdieh, Tabriz, Iran

Dedicated to the merciful angels who:

The lord of the worlds, who began to guide his servants with the teaching of the pen.

My parents, whose presence is a crown of honor for me and their name is a reason for my existence because these two existences after the lord, have been the source of my existence, took my hand and taught me to walk in this valley full of ups and downs.

Abstract

The subject of intellectual property is of great importance, so that by correctly or wrong analysis, the scope of property and property can be developed to the boundaries of intellectual property or separates between material and intellectual property. This thesis has been written in an analytical-analytical way, and we have come to the results that the result is a financial intellectual effect that has specific material and spiritual rights, and this property has been rational in addition to the usefulness of the rational. In contrast, there are also elders and jurists who either oppose the principle of property or the ownership of the creator to the work or the monopoly on its publication. The excellence of the contemporary jurisprudents of Imam Khomeini who opposed the monopoly of publishing the work, while accepting the ownership of the creator requires the right to appoint the owner, and this right is not only capable of the effect, but also to the carrier of the work. The domination of the carrier restricts the work. The intellectual work, including scientific, literary, artistic, invention, and the like, is considered property, and its objectivity, although not palpable in the material world, is meaningful in the universe and is tangible in a way that has external and unintended effects and today the most valuable property is the intellectual property that can be done impossible in the past, and is intended to violate the intellectual property in Imamiyyah jurisprudence based on jurisprudential rules.

Keywords: *Criminality, Violation, Intellectual Property, Imamiyyah Jurisprudence.*

Content

Chapter I

Introduction

Introduction

Intellectual property is a set of privileges and immunity and abilities that the creator of intellectual creation about immaterial and non -material. In today's world, an important part of property is intellectual property and is important to many. Because of the social reason, the impact of intellectual property in the development of knowledge and the provision of prosperity is very important. Economically, depending on the amount of thought production, the importance of that day expands and forms a significant and important part of the financial resources. Intellectual property is also very important politically. Because it is the formation of science from countries with high -production countries over the importing countries. Accepting the intellectual property system by assuming that there is intellectual production in the country is in the interests of the creator.

Because he can fully benefit from the economic benefits of his production, and this system is appropriate to the consumer's will and need. Because manufacturers and actors consider the scientific environment to be fully consumed by the consumer's demand. This is also in the direction of general materials and can accelerate the process of producing science. In the past, intellectual property debates in Islamic countries have been raised, but due to the insignificance of science and technology production, it has not been welcomed and in addition to the intellectual property debate in Islamic jurisprudence has not been discussed completely and independently.

Therefore, it is important to understand the legitimacy and place of intellectual property by ownership of non -material affairs in the Islamic legal system. Dr. Mir Hosseini quoted WiPu as saying intellectual property rights in the broad sense of the word rights arising from creations and intellectual creativity in the fields of scientific, industrial, literary and artistic.

Dr. Seyyed Hassan Emami, following the French Civil Code, has divided the property into two parts of material and immaterial and considers non-material property that has no material and objective existence abroad, but the society has credited its existence and the law recognizes it. It is, like the right to authorship, the right to compose and the patent. The importance of intellectual property is determined when its impact on business boom, especially international trade and technology research and development, especially new technologies, is discussed. The study of the effects of supporting assets and intellectual capital in the development of science and technology suggests that one of the major results of intellectual property support is to encourage scientists and researchers to conduct more and more effective research, as the reward against the genius of immune. In the field of international trade, the creation of advantage over competitors due to the ownership of intellectual capital by some market companions increases bargaining power and increased profits.

Criminalization can be defined as: criminalization is a process whereby the legislator, taking into account the basic norms and values of society, and relying on the theoretical basis, prohibits the current act or abandonment and guarantees criminal execution. he does. Accordingly, criminalization is a post-based and infrastructure sciences such as the philosophy of law, political philosophy, and social sciences. Some Imam Khomeini jurisprudents, including Imam Khomeini, do not accept sub -property rights. The basics of criminality violations of intellectual property in the sense of intellectual property in the Imamiyyah can be found in jurisprudential rules, including the rule of law and the principle of health. In this discussion, after providing explanations of key vocabulary and concepts and theoretical foundations, we examine the opponents and proponents of intellectual property in Imamiyyah jurisprudence for reasons and documentation, and then with jurisprudential rules to express criminality in intellectual property violations in Imamiyyah jurisprudence and executive guarantees. And we will be punished by the violators of these rights.

Chapter II

Concepts, Theoretical Foundations, and Research

Concepts:

Crime: Mass from the root of the mass means removing fruit from the tree. The word is metaphorically used to commit ugliness and commit sin. Crime means committing a crime and a criminal. The offender is the one who has fallen from the right to the right and the offender, the sinner.

The crime of action is contrary to the law of human beings, which is not the right to perform the assignments or the absence of the right, and there is a punishment for it. Criminalization can be defined as: criminalization is a process whereby the legislator, taking into account the basic norms and values of society and relying on the theoretical basis of their accepted, prohibits the current act or abandonment and guarantees criminal execution.

Accordingly, criminalization is a post -based and infrastructure sciences such as the philosophy of law, political philosophy, and social sciences.

Intellectual Property: The concept of ownership of the fake or noun means being owned. The word is both in the sense of property rights and seizures and the meaning of the property and object to which it belongs to. Property in jurisprudence means domination and monarchy, and ownership is an adjective used in this respect and is in fact rational credit. The intellect validates what is in the hands of someone who belongs to him, the interest between him and what he has at his disposal, which is the origin of his dominance.

The word thought or noun means thought that is a sum of thoughts, or that means thinking and reflection. Thus, intellectual property means all kinds of ownership and domination of intellectual effects for the creator of intellectual work. Legally, the term intellectual property refers to special rights and privileges over intellectual issues. In the United States, intellectual ownership includes rights created by copying, patent and trademark rights.

The copyright law gives the author an exclusive right to re -create, distribute, and adapt a literary, artistic or music work. The patent law gives the inventor the exclusive right to use, or sell the invention it has made, and the trademark law to the company gives the exclusive right to use a special mark or badge to identify its products.

Dr. Mir Hosseini considers intellectual property rights in the broad sense of the word rights caused by intellectual creativity and creativity in the fields of scientific, industrial, literary and artistic. Dr. Seyyed Hassan Emami, following the French Civil Code, has divided the property into two parts of material and immaterial and considers non-material property that has no material and objective existence abroad, but the society has credited its existence and the law recognizes. It is, like the right to authorship, the right to compose and the patent. Intellectual property rights are the rights that give its owners the right to benefit from human intellectual and innovative activities and have economic value and capability, but the subject is not a specific material object.

The rights of literary or artistic works or literary and artistic property known as the author or copyright right, patent, customer rights such as goodwill of businessmen and craftsmen in the name, commercial and industrial signs and commercial secrets known as commercial and industrial ownership It is intellectual ownership. Intellectual property is movable property that requires creativity or initiative and imagination and are commonly known as intellectual creatures. Copyright, trademarks, commercial secrets, and patents are all kinds of intellectual property. Some writers prefer the name of intellectual property for these rights. Because the source of these rights is human thought and thought, but others consider the word intellectual property more appropriate. Because some of these rights, such as goodwill, are not produced by thought, but only because they do not have material existence, they fall into the realm of these rights.

The common characteristics of the types of intellectual property are non -touch, exclusive, legal and limited to the particular area. Also, spiritual or intellectual right is a right other than objective and objective right, but a legal and non -material advantage that relates to the creator and to protect it, and gives its owner the exclusive authority of intellectual activity and initiative.

Imami jurisprudence: jurisprudence is used in the word to mean understanding, knowledge and cleverness. In the term, it also means knowledge of partial Shariah rulings or obtaining and knowing the obligatory practical duty from Shariah sources and evidence. Jurisprudence means to understand and understand, which helps to deduce the rulings of Sharia. Imami jurisprudence is one of the schools of jurisprudence in Islam. This religion is known as Shia jurisprudence because its followers are among the Shiites of the Twelve Imams, and it is also known as Jafari jurisprudence because it is very dependent on the sayings attributed to Jafar Sadiq, the sixth Imam of Shiites.

The sources of Shia jurisprudence are

- ✓ Quran.
- ✓ Hadith.
- ✓ Consensus.
- ✓ Intellect.

The sources through which one can obtain Sharia rulings are called evidences of rulings and sources of jurisprudence.

There are four Shia evidences

- ✓ Quran.
- ✓ Tradition.
- ✓ Consensus.
- ✓ Intellect.

Theoretical foundations:2-2- Theoretical bases of criminalization: In the Islamic legal system, punishment is to protect Islamic values and discipline and morally refine the criminal and ultimately create a healthy society through the prevention of social corruption.

For this purpose, each of the Islamic punishments has been legislated to protect individual rights or to protect public rights or both of them. Therefore, the reason of penal legislation refers to the philosophy of criminalization and punishments. In the implementation of punishment, Islam pursues multiple goals, all of which are aimed at the interests of humans.

The most important of these goals are

- ✓ Correctional education of criminals.
- ✓ Purification and education of criminals.
- ✓ Create deterrence.
- ✓ Implementation of criminal justice.

Criterion criteria: Accepted criteria for criminalization are different in each legal system. Therefore, in justifying the criminalization of a behavior, several criteria may be considered by the legislator. Human dignity, protection of moral values, negation of harm, preservation of basic interests, establishment of social order, implementation of criminal justice, prevention of crime are the criteria on which criminalization takes place. The Qur'an's approach in legislating penal regulations and criminalizing certain behaviors is aligned with these criteria.

Paying attention to human dignity: Man is the caliph of God and the worshiper of the angels, and this high position is combined with the capital of his dignity. Satan always tries to divert a person from the path of dignity and make him fall from his human position. Hazrat Ali has a beautiful and eloquent speech about this, which conveys the importance of human dignity: He who respects himself, despises whims and desires. The Holy Qur'an has repeatedly pointed out the high position of man and praised his status. Therefore, human beings and human society have inherent value, even though they have pests and deviations.

Beside this inherent value and dignity, there is an acquired dignity that is associated with the voluntary action of a human being. Because acquiring human virtues and observing piety in personal and social matters has a close relationship with human will and authority. Man is God's trustee and the world of creation is under his control. This superior being has reason and will and has the gift of speech and expression.

A being in whom the spirit of God has been breathed. Because of this status and dignity, it is a matter of respect, and the angels are prostrated by God. Human dignity requires paying attention to his intrinsic values. On the one hand, value and dignity are necessary to preserve the personality and rights of all human beings. Rights that no one can arbitrarily deny or limit, such as the right to life, both material and spiritual. According to the holy Qur'an, a human being has such a value that the life of a person is equal to the life of all human beings, and his death is equal to all human beings.

In the criminal system of Islam, respect for human dignity is provided by the criminalization of adultery and defamation. Regarding the wisdom of criminalizing adultery, it should be said: Crimes like murder may happen in public, but adultery is not like that. The fact that Islam is strict about the method of witnessing adultery is to support the family unit. Therefore, Islam has been strict both in punishing adultery and in the way of certifying and proving it. Both of these are for the same purpose, which is to support the institution of the family and preserve the chastity and chastity and dignity of individuals in social life. The author of tafsir Noor also writes under verse 23 of surah Yusuf, where he mentions prophet Yusuf's resistance to the request of his dear wife in Egypt: adultery is incompatible with human dignity.

Supporting moral values: Morality causes the collapse of the cohesion and structure of society. Along with legal moralism, human perfectionism and attention to moral values is also considered as a limiting principle of freedom and justifies the criminalization of some immoral behaviors. This theory is closer to the religious teachings and the view of the Holy Quran. It seems that the criminalization of crimes such as adultery and adultery has been done in order to support moral values. Of course, in this type of crimes, the negative consequences and their destructive effects on the institution of the family and its health are also considered. Because the satisfaction of the sexual instinct outside the family system causes the coldness of the family center and its collapse. The holy Qur'an has pointed out the ugliness and immorality of adultery and adultery and has considered such actions against human virtues and contrary to the way of good people.

Negation of harm: not harming others is seen in all legal systems, which is accepted by all thinkers and jurists with little difference. This principle is stated in Islamic law under the title of Harmless Rule. The rule of harm is in the fabric of Islamic criminal law. It can be safely said that no behavior is criminalized in Islam, unless that potential or actual behavior causes harm. This loss can be personal or social as well as material or spiritual.

The mentioned rule both removes the damage and repels the damage. In other words, it has both a remedial (constructive) function and a repulsive (deterrent) function. Most criminal laws prohibit antisocial behavior for causing harm to others, such as murder, assault, robbery, and arson. The guarantee of criminal execution in such cases is due to the loss itself. This type of criminalization refers to severe losses and direct damages, and the goals were prevented by other methods. The Qur'an has also criminalized severe damages and direct damages, but in cases of minor damages and self-harm, it has limited itself to sanctioning such acts or ordering civil guarantee and compensation.

This divine book has taken care to preserve human life and has criminalized intentional killing and wounding. In addition to a person's life, his honor and wealth are also very important. Also, personal comfort and social security have been emphasized by the Holy Quran and the violation of these values has been answered with criminal provisions.

Preservation of basic interests: Sharia rulings are subject to real interests and corruptions, and no ruling is imposed without criteria. In this regard, Imam Sadiq says: No ruling has been made without reason and criteria. Allama Hali writes in this context: All Shariah rulings are subject to interests, and interests also change with the change of time and the difference between the obligees. Therefore, it is possible that a certain ruling may be expedient for one person at one time and it is ordered, but it may be harmful for another person at another time and it is forbidden. Akhund Khorasani, referring to the obedience of God's commandments to benefits and harms, says: It is the opinion of Akhu that the rulings follow the real benefits and harms.

Master Martyr Morteza Motahari also writes about this: The laws of Islam, while being heavenly, are earthly and are based on the interests and corruptions in human life. Islam itself states that every law I have established is based on interests that are either related to your body or to your soul, of course, the interests are not always aligned with each other. Sometimes individual interests' conflict with each other and sometimes they collide with public interests.
This conflict occurs in every legal system, which is selected based on the important rule, so that in this way, balance and harmony can be established between individual rights and freedoms on the one hand, and public order and the interests of society on the other hand. Human life in its material and spiritual dimension is not possible except in the shadow of preservation and maintenance of these materials, and all Islamic laws are legislated to support these expedients. Different types of violation and violation of these materials create different types of crime.

Islam considers violation of valid human interests as a crime and organized criminalization in this regard. These human values and basic interests of the individual and society are

- ✓ Protection of people's health and life.
- ✓ Protection of people's reputation and dignity.
- ✓ Defense of generation and honor.
- ✓ Mental health.
- ✓ Protection of public property.
- ✓ Defense of private property.
- ✓ Ensuring people's comfort.
- ✓ Keeping the community safe.
- ✓ Respect for religious beliefs.
- ✓ Defending the ideals and value system of the society.

Establishing social order: The importance and necessity of social order is not hidden from anyone. The Holy Quran emphasizes the preservation of social order and considers it a necessity to eliminate chaos from human societies. Since crime is a violation of the social system, it contradicts the cultural rules and values of the society and hurts public feelings. Therefore, criminalization and execution of punishment will regulate relationships between people and establish order and security in society. Because if there is no order and security in a society and the rights of individuals are violated, the evolution of collective life will remain stagnant and the social life of people will be different. The penal system tries to outline the rights of individuals and society by announcing the list of crimes and their punishments, so that the importance of the values governing the society is known.

The existence of penal regulations that are carried out in the form of criminalization causes:

First: The scope of the crime should be determined, which will ensure the rights and freedoms of people better.

Secondly: The type and amount of punishment should be determined and the way to violence and coercion should be closed.

Thirdly: The way of execution of punishment by the legislator should be stated precisely, so that the field of arbitrariness and the exercise of taste are eliminated.

Therefore, establishing social order and avoiding chaos is one of the goals of criminal regulations. This point can be clearly understood in the legislation of retribution. Because determining the scope of retribution and the quality of its implementation by the Shariah will establish order and discipline in dealing with the crime of intentional murder. This prevents further revenge and bloodshed and makes dealing with the perpetrator of murder legal.

Implementation of criminal justice: justice is one of the principles that has been and still is important in legal systems. Since the criminal violated the norms by committing the crime and disturbed the moral order of the society, then justice requires the criminal to pay for his behavior and be punished. The Holy Qur'an has announced the establishment of installments and justice as one of the goals of the Prophets. On the one hand, it emphasizes the necessity of criminal laws and the punishment of criminals as a guarantee of justice.

Iron is a symbol of harshness and punishment, and defense tools are often made of this hard and strong material. Punishment legislation is in line with the fulfillment of the goals and ideals of divine prophets and for the implementation of justice so that criminals and violators of the rights of individuals and society reach their home of deeds and the ground for the expansion of justice and justice is provided. One of the most important aspects of criminalization and legalization of punishment in Islam is the administration of justice.

This function of punishment has long been the focus of legal schools, which is followed as punishment and punishment. It can be seen from the legislation of retribution that the Shariah has paid more attention to the execution of justice than anything else and has invited people to moderate the vindictiveness that the tribal society suffered from before Islam.

With the implementation of Islamic punishment, people better understand equality before the law and the observance of citizen's rights, and while feeling secure in the society, they trust and support the legal system and its governance more. Compensation for damages through the payment of ransom and equality in execution of retribution is mainly related to this aspect of the purpose of punishment. Because by executing the punishment, the injured people taste the taste of justice and regain their peace of mind.

Moderation in criminalization: The rules of the Qur'an are based on the axis of moderation, and this feature is reflected everywhere in this divine book. Moderation is the most important feature of the Islamic society that the holy Quran emphasizes. In the field of criminalization, observing moderation and avoiding excesses is the most obvious request and order of the Quran, and this fact can be clearly seen in the way of the implementation of the punishment for intentional homicide.

Just as neglecting public interests and the value system of the society is not acceptable and the legal system should not be lax in supporting them, excessive interference and maximum criminalization is not worthy of a wise and wise legislator. Because the criminal intervention limits the rights and freedoms of individuals and narrows its scope, and if criminalization exceeds the limit of necessity, the members of the society and the citizens of that government consider it an obstacle to their free activity. Basically, criminal law has a moral content and should be used in a measured manner.

It is appropriate that the criminal intervention be minimized and resort to coercion only in important cases and as much as necessary. Today, advanced criminal systems in the world have moved away from maximum criminalization and criminal inflation and have turned to the policy of decriminalization and decriminalization. In addition to minimal criminalization, these systems use correctional and educational solutions and protective and preventive measures to deal with crime and delinquency. While the Holy Qur'an presented a minimal criminalization system fourteen centuries ago and followed the path of moderation in legislating penal regulations.

Proportion of crime and punishment

One of the points that should be considered by the legislator in the process of criminalization is the observance of the proportionality between crime and punishment. Proportion and harmony between crime and punishment and its compliance by the legislator and law enforcers lead to the implementation of justice in the society and increase the acceptability of legal regulations in the eyes of the people of the society. Legal systems pay more attention to this rational principle in their evolutionary process and try to observe it as much as possible. Today, society's response to crime is more diverse, so that it can fit with the types of crimes and the personality of criminals, and be more successful in fighting crime and reforming criminals.

This is the same truth that can be seen in the penal laws of the Quran. Because this divine book has presented various moral and educational methods in the direction of reforming society and educating righteous people and has predicted various measures to deal with crime and delinquency. In the criminalization of moharebeh, we are also faced with this proportionality.

On the one hand, the type of punishment is related to deterring the criminal from repeating the crime and the prevalence of crime in the society. The discretion in choosing each of the four punishments is in line with the proportionality between the crime and the punishment, so that the rights of individuals and the interests of the society are better secured. For example, if a warrior has killed someone, it is appropriate to execute or impale him.

If he kidnapped Mali, it is more appropriate to cut off his hands and feet, and if he only pulled out the sword from Niam and scared the people, banishing such a person can be useful and effective. Because the exile of the criminal causes him to move away from the environment and exclude him from the society, which has the effect of intimidation and deterrence. In the criminalization of theft, the proportionality between crime and punishment is observed. Amputation of hands and feet in fighting and theft is done with the aim of disabling the criminal and it is proportional to the type of crime.

Theoretical foundations of intellectual property

Intellectual property rights are those legal privileges that allow the owners of thoughts to exclusively benefit from the fruits of their thoughts and creativity. The famous terms defining this type of rights are: the rights of new creations, intellectual rights, intangible property and intellectual property rights. Therefore, the word "rights" in this phrase means legal power and privilege. Therefore, intellectual property rights are rights that give the owner the exclusive right to benefit from human activity, thought, and initiative.

Today, these rights have expanded and diversified a lot with the help of custom and human societies, and it is not far from the mind that in the days to come, the examples of these rights will increase more and the financial and economic value of these properties will increase every day. The existence of the Internet alone is enough to make us think that materialism, meaning paying too much attention to material possessions, will become less prominent every day.

Intellectual property rights are divided into two main branches

1- Literary and artistic property rights or copyright: which includes all written and non-written works such as books, novels, plays, films, sculptures and other artistic and literary works, oral works and computer software.

2- Industrial property rights: which itself has sub-branches, such as patents, names and trademarks, geographical indications, trade secrets and industrial designs.

In terms of nature, these types of rights are not religious or personal rights. Because the right of the owner of the idea is not against a specific person. He is known as the owner of rights in front of everyone, like the owner of land or car. All society and even societies are prohibited from using the fruits of creative work of intellectual property right holders. Despite the difference of opinions that exist among jurists and despite the difference that exists between ordinary ownership and these rights, the belonging of these rights to individuals should be considered as ownership. Anyway, today intellectual property rights are divided into two general and major categories:

- ✓ **Literary and artistic property:** it is an exclusive and temporary right that the law has identified for the creators of works, such as the creators of literary or artistic works. In this branch of intellectual property rights, many financial and moral rights are recognized for the creator, including the reproduction and distribution of the work and its use to create other works and the translation of the work requires the permission of the author. According to different countries and conventions, these rights have a specific and valid and short life, which will remain for a maximum of 50 years after the death of the creator.
- ✓ **Industrial and commercial property:** This group of rights is related to those whose ideas are used in industry and commerce. Inventors and traders are the holders of these exclusive rights. An inventor is someone who creates a new process or discovery or device that has an industrial application in addition to being original. It is also possible for a

businessman to introduce his product or service by using a specific trade name or trademark that is registered according to the law in the authority of the Companies and Industrial Property Registration Office in accordance with the regulations. The right to exclusive use of this trademark or trade name belongs to the businessman, but he can assign this financial right for free or in return. Also, industrial designs and forms, trade secrets and technical know-how are other examples of industrial and commercial property rights.

Characteristics of intellectual property rights: The discussed set of rights, despite their great differences, have common characteristics that distinguish them from other properties. Immateriality of property rights Since ancient times, what humans have considered as property has been material property. Among the properties, nobles, and finally, among the nobles, immovable property has had an extraordinary amount.

This difference in the customary view of the value of property has resulted in many legal effects, but in the last two centuries, properties with other economic values have gradually emerged, which were not considered before. In terms of wealth, immaterial properties are no different from other properties and gradually become more valuable in the world. The most important feature of intellectual property rights is that it does not belong to material and tangible property.

What is considered as right and property are fertile and crystallized ideas that sometimes appear as works and sometimes as innovations and inventions. Rights support the crystallized thought itself in the outside world as the right of the inventor or creator. Doubts about the ownership or ability to collect these properties are due to this prominent feature of intangible property. One of the results of the immateriality of these properties is that their use does not cause deterioration and destruction of their owner's properties. In addition, unlike material possessions, many people can use their fruits at the same time.

The exclusivity of intellectual property rights: all examples of the discussed rights are exclusive and special. In other words, these rights are created so that their owners have the opportunity to use them alone, but it is obvious that this opportunity becomes meaningful when the society is demanding and willing to use that exclusive knowledge and information. The extent of this usefulness makes the financial value of these properties clear. The exclusivity of these rights, from another point of view, brings them negative. This means that the patent owner or author has the right to prohibit everyone from exploiting his property. However, in some cases, the possibility of imposing the will of society on the owner of the right to surrender his rights is foreseen. Also, one of the effects of the exclusivity of the aforementioned rights is the ability to invoke them in front of everyone. A description that makes them very close to objective rights.

Temporality of intellectual property rights: According to the rule that the free exchange of information is essential for the development of human societies and the interest of society lies in simple and easy access to information and knowledge, the rights in question have a short validity. Although this period is different based on the countries and examples of the discussed rights and governing conventions, it is limited anyway and compared to the ownership of nobles and especially immovable property, it is very short. The time limitation of the discussed rights keeps them away from the concept of ownership and the questionable description of the obligation in the institution of waqf. These rights are based on knowledge and information. There is no precise definition of information, but without a doubt, every information and knowledge does not have financial value. Not only are thoughts alone not supported, but information and knowledge outside the mind is not supported at all.

Today's world is the age of information, and the value of information and access to information is very high, and wherever information is considered valuable, the rights in question will be more respected and respected. All types of rights discussed are based on knowledge and information. This, in turn, implies works.

Globalization of these rights: Due to the fact that the existence of these rights is based on knowledge and information, and these matters are the means of work and the necessity of the survival and life of all societies, much faster than their recognition, we see the expansion of respect and esteem for them from a We are on the other hand, creating unity in their regulations at the international level through the conclusion of conventions and treaties, including the regulations of the World Trade Organization. This feature in turn brings results.
Continuity and close connection of the exchange of these rights with world trade is clearly evident in the biggest regulations of the World Trade Organization, which include international conflicts caused by the violation of the rights of citizens of other countries. At the end of this discussion, it is necessary to point out that the recognition and respect of these rights, which have an extraordinary economic and commercial value in creating the national income of countries, is very necessary, and having such privileges and monopolies is undoubtedly one of many It is not considered less valuable than nobles. It is also useful to mention that there are other common aspects among these rights that are avoided in their discussion.

The importance of promoting and spreading intellectual property:
Intellectual property is to today's businesses what oxygen in the air is to humans. The survival of businesses depends on intellectual assets and their protection, and as a result, the prosperity and progress of humanity is undeniably dependent on intellectual property rights. Experts and experts in the field of intellectual property mention several key reasons for the importance of promoting and spreading this matter:

- ✓ The progress of societies and public welfare depends on the ability and ability to create and develop technological innovations and cultural works that are directly related to intellectual property.
- ✓ Legal support and protection of new works and inventions increases investments with the aim of further innovation.

- ✓ Promotion and protection of intellectual property leads to economic growth, job creation, formation of new industries and increase in quality of life.

An efficient and fair intellectual property system helps countries to benefit from the potential of intellectual property as a catalyst for economic development, social welfare and cultural promotion. The intellectual property system helps to balance the interests of innovators and public interests and provides an environment where creativity and innovation become a public value in society.

Types of intellectual property: According to intellectual property sources and authorities, such as the World Intellectual Property Organization, the United States Patent and Trademark Office, and the text of international treaties and conventions, intellectual property rights can be placed in several distinct categories. Each of these classes refers to a specific type of intellectual property and has unique characteristics.

- ✓ Patent certificate.
- ✓ Trademarks.
- ✓ Industrial designs.
- ✓ copy right.
- ✓ Geographical signs.
- ✓ Trade secrets.

Intellectual property and international treaties: In recent decades, intellectual property has become a key issue in the economy and other areas of human life. With the increase in communication between different societies and the globalization of businesses, a series of international treaties and conventions have been created in the field of intellectual property protection, the most important of which are the paris convention for the protection of Industrial property (1883), the berne convention for the protection of Literary works and henry (1886), the Madrid agreement for the protection of trademarks (1891), the Hague agreement for the protection of industrial designs (1925) and the TRIPS agreement on commercial aspects of Intellectual property rights.

History of intellectual property

Since the beginning of human creation, according to his nature and nature, he valued his little or big efforts and he used to enjoy what he got and prevented others from taking it, so that this instinctive feeling originated in human beings. Personal savings and a sense of belonging have been given to them. This feeling is not only limited to his occult collections, but also applies to the poems he writes, the paintings he draws, or the things he writes. According to some people, ever since man was able to hold a pen or a brush, there has been this feeling that there are many cases from ancient times in this case. For example, Plato's student Humodorus took his notes to Sicily and sold them there. This act, which was done without Plato's permission, was not only praised by the people of science and literature, but also provoked the anger of the people.

In Europe, this discussion clearly started during the Renaissance era and with the intellectual-industrial revolution that appeared there, especially in the printing industry, and the first works of support for writings should be sought in the privileges that European rulers and sultans gave to publishers in the 16th century and the booksellers donated, which made the publishers and printers consider these rulings as a means to encroach on the authors' rights.

This situation continued for two centuries in Europe until, for the first time, in 1709 in England, a law was approved by the queen, which officially recognized the rights of the authors of the work. At the beginning of this century, a law on the same subject was approved in France, and little by little many other countries in Europe, Latin America and Asia began to establish such laws. At the end of the 19th century, with the expansion of communications and the progress of astronomical sciences and industries, it became clear that even though national laws are not comprehensive and complete, they cannot properly defend the moral rights of authors and inventors.

Because abusers commit literary, artistic and industrial thefts outside the national borders with the help of mass communication devices. Therefore, bilateral and multilateral and finally international agreements were provided in this field, until in the field of industrial property and the rights of inventors, it reached the Paris Convention of 1883 for the protection of industrial property, which had 140 members until 1996, and in the field of the rights of the authors of literary and artistic works and Science also led to the Swiss Bern Convention in 1886.

By merging the offices of these two international conventions in 1893, the first foundation stone of the world Intellectual property organization was laid. In the history of Islamic civilization, learning, reading and writing has been a religious necessity and the prophet of Islam has raised the call of science as a value from the very first days, but the discussion of the origin of the book in the Islamic world in particular has a deep connection with the writing of hadith, which in terms of Shariah has a great responsibility and its validity also depends on the Shariah of the carrier. Therefore, not every book was accepted by everyone, and the personality of the author was an issue.

At the end of the second century and the formation of the translation movement in which many scientific and intellectual achievements from Greece, Rome, Iran, India and other conquered nations were translated into Arabic. Writing, gilding, binding, and copying have become advanced and lucrative professions, and the ground for forging, distorting, or misrepresenting the translation of others has arisen during copying, but because of the government's support for translators and the fact that many are in the service of the government.

From the copyists to send multiple copies to other parts of the country, this was under control and happened less often. On the other hand, believing that the expansion of religious sciences and knowledge is a shari'a duty, most of the authors or translators either did not pay attention to the material rights resulting from it or were satisfied with the same amount of government reward, but they recognized the right that the work belongs to them. He considered it reserved for himself, and some even expressed it. In Iran, the first literary ownership contract between Iran and

Germany was concluded in ۱۹۳۰, and its first legal approaches are also in Chapter 11 of the Criminal Code on conspiracy and fraud in acquisition approved in ۱۹۳۱.

Chapter III

The arguments of opponents and supporters of intellectual property in Imami jurisprudence:

The nature of intellectual property in Imami jurisprudence:

Ownership is a social, economic, and legal institution that in all societies, governments, and legal systems implies the highest level of rights that can be imagined in relation to an object. This institution has two functions, one is that the society allows the individual to use resources, and the second is that the individual has the authority over others to determine how to use that resource. From an economic point of view, ownership is the practical possibility of benefiting from a property regardless of how it is obtained, but from a legal point of view, the method of obtaining it is important and must be legal. The nature of ownership has been defined according to two traditional and new theories.

In the traditional theory, ownership is the relationship between the owner and the owned object. A relationship that establishes the highest level of authority for the owner in relation to that object. In jurisprudence, this theory is also accepted, which means that the relationship between the owner and the mamluk, the owner's sovereignty over the mamluk or a special interest that is the origin of the aforementioned monarchy, the validity of the ownership of the owner over the mamluk and the validity of the owner's sovereignty over the mamluk, which in all these views is the authority of a person considered on the object.

In this regard, Imam Khomeini says: Ownership means added credit and assignment between a person called malik and an object called mamluk. Also, in the traditional field, the view of shahid Motahari can be expressed: ownership is a matter of credit that humans have assumed by adapting it from the real world. What man understands about ownership in the outside world is the ownership that exists between him and his thoughts, actions, powers and members, but like this relationship between himself and objects that are the product of nature or the product of work and nature or the product of work and nature and It is capital, it assumes that it expands its existence in the world of credit and considers it valid according to the social contract, and based on this ratio, it gives itself the right to make any possession of it or even destroy it.

The important point regarding the traditional theory is that ownership is a right that is attached to an object, and unlike other financial rights where the separation between the right and the object of its subject is completely obvious, ownership is intertwined with its subject. For this reason, they sometimes consider ownership instead of financial rights and consider other rights to be lesser and weaker.

With this interpretation, what is acquired, legal possession and transfer is the credit relationship between a person and an object, not the object itself. The traditional theory considers ownership as the relationship between the owner and the owned object, but in the new theory, ownership is a series of relationships between people regarding an object.

The property right in the new theory is a set of relationships, rights and mutual obligations between persons subject to the right to a specific object. For example, a person who owns a car has different rights, duties and relationships regarding the ownership of his car compared to other people. His property right is a combination of rights, claims, privileges, powers and immunities. On the other hand, this person has obligations to the general public, such as having a driver's license or not speeding. Traditionalists attach a fundamental role to the object of ownership, while supporters of the new theory consider the legal relationship between persons regarding the object of ownership to be more important. In the framework of the traditional approach to ownership, intellectual property is a relationship established between the creator as the owner and the intellectual work as the owner. Since the ownership relationship has always existed between people and tangible objects since the distant past, accepting such a relationship between people and intangible objects such as intellectual works that are independent of any material origin is difficult in the opinion of many who say the traditional theory of ownership. According to the theory of rights, intellectual property refers to the rights, privileges, powers and immunities that the creator has against others regarding the intellectual work. His rights are due to the intellectual work that creates duties and obligations for others. In addition to these rights and privileges, they also have duties and obligations. Therefore, with the theory of rights, intellectual property rights are more acceptable.

Types of property and ownership: types of property cannot be considered separately from types of property, but ownership has different types according to the owner and the type of creation. Jurists and jurists have divided the right into two types: the right to usufruct and the right to own. The right to an intellectual work cannot be the right of usufruct, because the right of usufruct is a right by which a person can use property that is the same property of another or does not have a specific owner. In other words, as a result of a contract or agreement, the owner of the usufruct can only use the property that has been placed at his disposal, without being the actual owner or owner of the property.

Comparison between beneficial ownership and usufruct

First: The benefit or benefits are considered to be the property of the owner, such as the rental of the property and the interest during the rental period are the property of the lessee, while the usufructuary right holder is only allowed to use the property and this right is not considered among his assets.

Second: The beneficial owner has the right to rent it to someone else, but the usufructuary does not have such a right.

Third: If the owner of the benefits dies, the benefits will go to his heirs, but if the owner of the usufruct dies, the usufruct will be terminated, and in fact, the usufruct is based on the person.

Fourth: If someone usurps the benefits from the owner, he must compensate the owner of the benefits. For example, the person who usurped the property leased by the tenant must pay the damage to the tenant, but for the usufructuary, if damage is caused to the property, the damage will not be paid to him, and the owner of the property has the right to receive the damage.

With these explanations, the right to an intellectual work should be considered a property right. Now we will examine the types of ownership to determine the ownership position of the intellectual work.

Objective ownership and benefit: the civil law considers ownership to be specific to nobles and interests, and article 29 is dedicated to this issue. Article 29 states: People may have the following interests in property. Ownership (whether for purpose or benefit), right of usufruct, right of easement to another's property. The ownership of the owner of an intellectual work should be considered objective ownership, because the external object is not exclusive to material property, and immaterial property is also tangible, but according to human reason and feeling, not physical tangible, and an example of that is poetry, which human reason and feeling, existence and beauty.

He feels and understands it. In the field of intellectual property rights, beneficial ownership is also envisaged and current for the parties to the contract of assigning the material rights of the work, such as publishers and producers of motion pictures and the like. This ownership is like the ownership of interest in material property, which, of course, has its own limits according to the law. For example, according to article 14 of the Law on the protection of the rights of authors, writers and artists, the maximum transfer of beneficial ownership in literary, scientific and artistic works is thirty years, or according to article 13 of the said law, the beneficial ownership of a commissioned work is a maximum of thirty years from the date of creation to order.

The donor is transferred and it is also in the case of cinematographic and photographic works and cases belonging to legal entities where this thirty-year limitation exists in the transfer of beneficial ownership. In all cases, ownership returns to the owner of the work.

Primary and secondary ownership: Primary ownership is that which was created without precedent and includes two types of primary and secondary ownership. The main ownership is that which is not created through and as a result of ownership of something else, such as the possession of free objects and the restoration of favorable land, river water or fishing from the sea, but the secondary ownership is that which originates from and as a result of another ownership. has been, such as ownership of the fruits and results of property.

Ownership of intellectual works is the type of primary ownership, because the reason for owning intellectual works is compatibility and homogeneity with the revival of favorable lands and possession of laudable objects. In other words, the same logic and nature prevails in the field of intellectual property. Science, literature and concepts are all present in the world of existence, and some people with their effort, taste, innovation and knowledge discover some of them and make them public, or with their own initiative and taste, they use some concepts and words to convey scientific and philosophical concepts or they use literature and actually revive it.

Hafez's or Rumi's or any other poet's poetry is not the creation of concepts and words, but the beautiful and accurate use of concepts and words. The owner of the intellectual work has actually revived the concepts and words that already existed and that everyone could use, and took possession of them with taste and innovation. The endless expansion of the field of science, literature and art from the distant past to the ages and future centuries prevents the creation of limitations and narrowing of the field of innovation and creativity, and for this reason, it has an important advantage over the revival of favorable lands and even the fishing of seas and oceans.

The result is that the ownership of an intellectual work is one of the examples of original ownership, and the rights arising from it, including the right to publish, the right to present in the form of film, music, performance and display, digital and virtual space, are the same as the fruits and results of material property that are created for the owner. However, regarding secondary ownership that is taken from others, such as inheritance and sale, two types of forced and optional ownership can be counted. Forced ownership, such as inheritance, is transferred from one person to another person or persons without specific authority and will, and this type of ownership is also conceivable and available in intellectual property rights.

In this regard, the following points should be considered

The first point: ownership in intellectual works includes two groups of rights, one group of material rights and the other group of intellectual rights. Each of these two groups has only one of the two important principles of permanent ownership and transferability according to the law and according to the legislative wisdom. Intellectual rights are permanent but non-transferable and material rights are transferable and non-permanent. Therefore, regarding coercive ownership and the discussion of inheritance, intellectual rights cannot be inherited by anyone, but material and financial rights are considered coercive rights.

The Second point: The validity of material rights for the creator is limited to his lifetime and up to fifty years after his death. It is natural that with the expiration of this period, according to the expediency of legislation, no right remains for the executor or heir, and while the intellectual rights are still reserved for the creator, but the material rights are freed and everyone can publish the work under the supervision of the Islamic ruler.

The third point: It is not only primary ownership that is inherited by force, but also secondary ownership may be inherited upon the death of the owner, i.e., publisher or producer.

The second type of secondary ownership is discretionary ownership that is created and transferred by will and intention, such as sale, peace and gift. The transfer of material rights of an intellectual work and the conclusion of a publishing contract creates discretionary ownership for the publisher. The point to be mentioned here is that secondary ownership, which is intended for the publisher or producer of the artwork, has two types of time limits.

First, according to articles 13 and 14 of the Law on the Protection of the Rights of authors, writers and artists, the transfer of material rights, or in other words, the right of secondary ownership of the publisher or producer, if a shorter period is not agreed upon, is a maximum of thirty years from the time of transfer, and after that the ownership the secondary is ruled out and the same primary ownership prevails for the creator.

The second type of limitation is the subordination of the secondary ownership to the primary ownership after the death of the creator, and the secondary ownership is lost after fifty years of the death of the owner of the work at the same time as the termination of the primary ownership. In other words, if the heirs of the creator sign a publishing contract with the publisher after, for example, thirty years after his death, and do not set a time limit, the publisher only has permission to publish exclusively for twenty years, and his contract with the heirs of the author of the work is valid, and after with the termination of the primary ownership right of the author of the work, the secondary ownership right of the publisher is also terminated.

Private, public and government ownership: in the science of law, ownership has been divided into three categories. Private ownership, public ownership and government ownership. The main and most comprehensive type of ownership is related to natural persons. Private ownership is older than other types of ownership. First, man as an individual took possession of things, and little by little, with the formation of society and government, he took things out of private ownership and brought them under public or government ownership.

Private ownership drives the scientific, cultural, economic and social life of society and public and government institutions are obliged to protect and strengthen it. This is the description of a society that takes the path of progress and excellence and approaches progressive goals. Ownership is not a single right, but it is a package of rights, both positive and negative, which on the one hand the owner considers entitled to rights, such as the right to possession, the right to use, the right to transfer and any kind of treatment with the property, and on the other hand the owner It prevents it from some things. Such as excessive use, harm to others, abuse of rights, and in a word, responsibility towards others.

The basis of private ownership is a natural or legal person, and other than that, they are all levels of public ownership. In other words, private property is absolute and fixed and without different assumptions, but public property has many levels and divisions. Legal entities in today's modern societies aggregate the private property of individuals and partners, but at the same time, the ownership share of individuals is clear and definite. The public area can be explained by some things, for example, according to the law of ownership of apartments, private and common areas are defined and rules have been established for each of them.

Therefore, within an apartment complex, both private and public ownership are defined, and some items are designated as public ownership in a common way for the owners of the units, and they can benefit in some cases in proportion to the value of shares and in some cases equally.

This ownership is public for the owners of the complex, but it is considered private for the members of the society and other people. In other words, things that are subject to public ownership in an apartment complex are subject to private ownership in relation to society. According to the city or country, public property is defined and people outside that city or country are not allowed to use public property. Today, assuming the absence of humans in other worlds and planets, public ownership is limited to the earth and cannot be developed at the moment. Therefore, based on international rules and regulations, spaces and boundaries have been designated as public property for all people on the planet, such as oceans and seas. Iran's civil law in 1928 tried to determine criteria for public ownership. Articles 24 and 25 of this law stated as follows:

Article 24: No one can own public roads and alleys whose ends are not blocked.

Article 25: No one can own property that is used by the public and does not have a specific owner, such as bridges, caravanserais, public reservoirs, old schools, and public squares, as well as canals and wells that are used by the public.

Also, the Constitution of the Islamic Republic of Iran explains public property in the 45th principle:
The 45th principle: Anfal and public wealth such as favorable or abandoned lands, mines, seas, lakes, rivers and other public waters, mountains, valleys, forests, reeds, natural groves, pastures that are not private, inheritance without heirs and unknown property. The property and public property that is returned from the usurpers is at the disposal of the Islamic government to act on them according to the public interest. The law determines the details and order of using each one.
But state ownership is not the ownership of properties that the public can use, such as parks and streets, but the government as a sovereign has all the characteristics of an owner and has the same package of rights that we mentioned in private ownership, such as large steel factories, iron smelting and automobile manufacturing.

Article 26 of the Civil Law refers to this type of ownership
Article 26: State property that is reserved for public purposes or benefits, such as fortifications, castles, ditches, military embankments, barracks, weapons, reserves, and warships, as well as furniture, buildings, state buildings, state telegraph wires, museums, and public libraries.
Historical monuments and their like, including movable and immovable property that the government has under its possession as public goods and national interests, cannot be privately owned, as well as property that has been assigned to the state, province, district or city in accordance with the public interest.
After stating the types of ownership, it is necessary to check which group intellectual property belongs to and which type of ownership intellectual property should be included in. Intellectual property is basically in the domain of private property, and this, in addition to the fact that, like the rest of the property, privacy has priority, the intellectual nature of this property and the exclusive ability to assign these works to a real person is another reason an intellectual work is the

product of the mind's effort, and the mind is only imagined in a real person, and a legal person cannot create a work in any way.

Of course, it should be known that the meaning of intellectual property here is the initial ownership of the intellectual work resulting from its creation, not the subsequent stages of ownership and intermediaries that can provide the means of its transfer. Some jurists have referred to the issue of ordering the work or employment, to prove the ownership of the government and legal entities, which seems to be out of the question, because in intellectual property, it means the original ownership of the work, which is caused by its creation, not whether can the initial ownership be transferred to someone else, be it natural or legal persons or not?

Of course, intellectual property, like other properties, can be owned by natural and legal persons and can be donated for public use. Regarding the work resulting from the order, where the ordering party may be a legal entity, or the work resulting from employment, which is usually the employer of the legal entity, it should be noted that the ownership of the work is primarily private, as well as the intellectual rights of the work, even in the case of assigning material rights, is fixed and reserved for the creator.

In the case of ordering a work, as soon as the agreement is reached, the material rights of the work and its material ownership are transferred to the client, and in the case of the employment of the creator, the agreement of the parties is sufficient for the subject of the agreement that he hands over the ownership of the work to the employer in exchange for regular rights. In both cases, the issue of transfer of primary and original ownership is raised, and the nature of both cases is the usual and common transfer and transfer of ownership.

Therefore, the principle of intellectual property is private, and public and public property is obtained through private ownership. In addition to government ownership, a public institution or organization may enter into a contract with the owner of the work to receive the material rights of an intellectual work and offer it to the public to help educate or acquaint citizens with their rights and duties. In this way, the mentioned work is placed in the public domain and the general citizens can use the information or the work presented in the physical or virtual space. Of course, this transfer to the public still includes a thirty-year limit from the time of transfer, and after that the material rights are transferred from the public to the person who owns the work.

This type of public intellectual works is abundantly seen in advanced societies, but another issue in this regard is related to the compulsory and legal entry of intellectual works into the domain of public ownership. According to article 12 of the Law on the Protection of the rights of authors, authors and artists, the material rights of the intellectual work are reserved for him and his executors and heirs for a maximum of fifty years after the death of the creator, and after that, these rights are released and everyone can use them by observing and preserving the rights. The author's intellectual property is to publish and exploit the material rights of the work.

Some jurists believe that in the above-mentioned conditions, the intellectual work enters the public sphere, rather than becoming public property, and they have argued that the characteristic of public property is the ability to use and exploit it for the people of a particular society or country, not for the general public, therefore an intellectual work does not become public property and only enters the public domain. On the other hand, it is in this situation that when the force of the law is removed, the rarity element is lost and the intellectual work is removed from being property.

It seems that this theory is facing many problems

First: After fifty years after the death of the creator, the intellectual work really becomes public property. Public ownership with the same definition and nature as for material property an important condition that was proposed for public ownership is public use without the possibility of establishing monopoly and preventing the use of others. This condition really exists in the intellectual work we are discussing and according to the law, the monopoly of its use and exploitation is excluded. It is not accurate to say that in public property, the owners are the people of the society or the country and others cannot use it, while as a result of thinking, by entering the public domain, all people in the world can benefit from it, because the principle of public property is Emphasis on the ownership of both material and intellectual property belongs to the same society or country, but the use of property that has become public property is permitted and unobstructed for the people of the world, whether it is material property or intellectual property.

For example, a public park in a city, although it is owned by the same community or country, foreigners cannot be prohibited from entering it. This story is also true for the intellectual property for which public ownership is created, because the principle of ownership is related to the administration and supervision of the relevant government of the country, while the general public of the world can use this work and benefit from its material benefits.

Secondly: The argument that rarity is one of the two conditions for property of an intellectual work with the help of the law has fundamental problems. As it was said before, the publication of the work does not cause the loss of the element of rarity in order to arrive at a rarity factor such as law.

Thirdly: It has been said that every object needs two elements of utility and rarity to be property, while ownership only requires the element of rarity, and a work that has passed fifty years since the death of its creator and the use of its material rights has been freed, has been lost. The element has become rare and therefore will no longer be a property. The answer is that an intellectual work is both property and property, and this is because it has the element of usefulness and rarity, and its reproduction and dissemination does not affect its nature.

This private ownership, both materially and spiritually, continues for fifty years after the creator's death, until the legislator only cancels the monopoly on the material rights of the work and makes these material rights public property so that the public can publish and reproduce them. Pay other uses of material rights. Now, why does the legislator make this transformation and transform the private ownership of the material rights of the work into public ownership, it is because the creator is a self-cultivated human society and has sat at the table of science and knowledge and human experience since birth, and of course He has gained new achievements with his efforts. The legislator has considered the intellectual rights to be fixed for him forever and the material rights have been protected in addition to his lifetime up to fifty years after his death, and after that he has given them the basic services of the society and with the aim of expanding the sciences that have passed more than it is still attractive and effective for fifty years, Azad has made it. The result is that after fifty years after the death of the creator, the intellectual work does not fall from property due to the lack of the element of rarity which the law is responsible for, but first of all from the point of view of intellectual rights of property and ownership, the work is permanent and from the point of view of material rights according to article 12 of the law protecting the rights of authors, authors and artists, the private property of the creator becomes public property.

Arguments of opponents of intellectual property rights

The reasons that the opponents of the legitimacy of intellectual property rights cite to prove their opinion are: the incompatibility of intellectual property with the rule of sovereignty, the lack of signature of such rights by the Shariah, the incompatibility of intellectual property rights with the mission and sanctity of science and the impossible. Personal possession is this category of rights. Among the Shia scholars, Imam Khomeini's arguments and ideas are mostly considered in the field of opposition to intellectual property rights, and we will examine these reasons below.

The incompatibility of intellectual property rights with the rule of sovereignty:

Imam Khomeini considers the emergence of any exclusive right to use intellectual works for its creators as against the rule of sovereignty, and they say that what is called natural right by some people is not a Shariah right and deprives people of control. It is not allowed on their property without any kind of contract. Therefore, just printing a book and writing the words of copyright and imitation is reserved for its owner, it does not cause anything and it is not considered an agreement with others. Therefore, it is permissible for someone else to print and copy it, and it is not permissible for anyone to prevent him from doing so. In the justification of this matter, it is stated that intellectuals do not agree on the fact that a right is created for the owner of the printing house as soon as the book is printed.

Also, there is no definite consensus on banning people from imitating, because people's nature is based on imitation in all matters, actions, inventions, and professions, and it is reasonable to imitate in one of the industrial affairs and make an object from another example and benefit from the result. They do not consider the thought of the past to be a usurpation of the rights of others, which is subject to the permission of the owners of these industries, actions and thoughts, and book printing is not out of the flow of this tradition.

Non-signing of intellectual property rights by the Shariah: Some jurists are against the legitimacy of such rights with the argument that the intellectual property rights have not been signed and validated by the Shariah.

Ayatollah Safi Golpayegani writes in this regard: I have not been able to reconcile copyright, authorship and patent rights in the sense defined in the new laws and the works that result from them with Islamic rules and systems. It is not about the contracts and transactions that we can say, although it was not mentioned in the age of the sacred Shariah, but it is considered to be a contract and transaction, considering the conditions that are valid in the validity of the contract and transaction. In the criticism of the opinion mentioned above, it can be said that firstly, although there were inventions and innovations in the time of Shariah, and at the same time intellectual property rights were not mentioned, it is not considered an obstacle to the recognition of these rights in our time.

In the olden days, intellectual and cultural works had a limited scope and scope, and the authors did not expect material exploitation of their works. Therefore, legal protection of such works was not necessary, but in today's world the situation has completely changed. The expansion of intellectual creations and their sensitive role in the development of culture, civilization and human economy has caused the legislators to be indifferent to the intellectual rights of the owners of intellectual works and audio-visual productions.

However, the existence of some rights does not negate their legitimacy. Protecting the environment today is considered one of the Muslim rights of the members of the society, and governments set fines and punishments for those who pollute the environment. It cannot be said that because such a right did not exist at the time of Sharia, it is not legitimate even today. In previous ages, lives were simple and cities were much less populated than in our time. There was no news about polluting factories.

It is not possible to compare this period with the previous ages and delegitimize it due to the fact that the issue of environmental protection was not raised in those ages. Secondly, as some jurists have said, buildings that are rationally based on their nature and substance, such as intellectually based on telephone franchise, goodwill, and authorship rights, do not need to be signed and verified until the time of infallibility. Also, this right cannot be considered as a customary right, like the right of precedent or the right of subrogation, and it can be considered legitimate based on this. Because it is correct to adhere to custom and the foundation of reason in a place where the Sharia has signed the customary method, in the event that despite the existence of the author, innovator and inventor, no right has been established for them in the age of Sharia.

Incompatibility of intellectual property rights with the mission and sanctity of science: among Sunni scholars, some have opposed it with the argument that intellectual property is incompatible with the mission and sanctity of science from the point of view of Islam. From the point of view of these people, considering this right as valid causes the restriction and imprisonment of scientific works and the concealment of knowledge, which is prohibited by the holy Quran.

The holy prophet also said: whoever knows knowledge and hides it, he will be brought from the fire on the Day of Judgment. In the criticism of the opinion mentioned above, it can be said that, although Islam attaches special value and dignity to science and knowledge, but from the point of view of Islam, taking money and earning money with any holy matter is forbidden and not permissible.

Apart from this, hiding science and making money through scientific works are two completely different things. In fact, what is forbidden in the narration of the Prophet is the concealment of knowledge and not earning money through scientific activities. In other words, the prohibition of concealment of science does not require that the owners of scientific works give up their material rights or that people are not required to respect their rights.

As prohibition of hoarding does not mean free supply of hoarded goods. Using intellectual works without the permission of their creators will be an example of falsehood and violation of people's rights. Acknowledging the exclusive right of publishing for the creator leads to the concealment of knowledge and, in addition, the negation of its religious aspect, while based on numerous narrational evidences, God and His Prophet dislike the concealment of knowledge and a purely materialistic attitude towards it.

Intellectual property rights cannot be acquired by individuals: some thinkers consider intellectual property rights as public wealth, which cannot be acquired by individuals. Shahid Motahari writes: Man owes his physical and mental powers to the community, and those powers and forces are not only his own, but the community has the right to them. These are not infringements of individual property, but the abolition of private property. In these cases, ownership is shared and social, just as in Islam, anfal is considered public wealth. In criticizing the opinion mentioned above, it can be said that firstly, the claim that the works of intelligence and genius cannot have a personal owner is a claim without reason. Secondly, although the society plays a significant role in the flourishing of intellectual creations and people create intellectual works by using the facilities of the society, but this does not mean that a person does not become the owner of his intellectual works.

Of course, in order to respect the right of the society, the exclusive right of use of the creator of the work can be limited to a certain period of time, after which the use period will be released to the public.

Arguments of supporters of intellectual property rights

Many contemporary jurists agree with the legitimacy of intellectual property rights. Some of them only mentioned the creation of exclusive right for the creator of the work, but they did not mention the basis of the ruling. On the other hand, some others have also mentioned the basis of the verdict. The reasons for the legitimacy of this category of rights are: transferable evidence, rational basis, the rule of sovereignty, the sanctity of taking possession of other people's property without their permission, the rule of harm, the solution of the authority of the jurist, the interests of the sender, and the restriction of resources. We will review them below:

Narrative proofs

Among the narrated proofs are the verses and hadiths that indicate the sanctity of using people's property without their consent, the obligation to keep agreements, the importance of acquiring knowledge, the sanctity of usurping and violating the rights of others. Negation of harm, difficulty and embarrassment with the assumption that this right is considered a kind of property. It is among the most important documents of the supporters of the legitimacy of intellectual property rights. Among the other supporting documents from among the Sunni jurists, especially from the point of view of the objectives of the Sharia, is the evidence of the interests of the sender and also the custom, which are cited especially regarding the legitimacy of the author's right, and it is in accordance with the goals and objectives of the Sharia in preserving the sanctity of the property and rights of others. They know the publication of knowledge.

The building of reason

One of the arguments mentioned for the legitimacy of intellectual property rights is the building of reason. Some jurists consider the rights of intellectual property as a Shari'a right, citing the basis of rationality. Some Shia jurists have also tried to prove the legitimacy of the author's right by insisting on reason as a source of deriving rulings. With the explanation that rational reasons such as the need to preserve the system of Islamic society and the need to meet the needs of Muslims require that the system of intellectual property rights be accepted. Because the removal of this legal system causes disruption in the livelihood of a number of people, chaos, hardship and embarrassment and endangering people's property and diseases.

In addition, the acceptance of the system of property rights of intellectual works leads to strengthening the motivation of individuals in creating new works, which are among the interests of Muslims. The proponents have also cited the reason of the building of aqla and said that due to the prevalence of this practice, i.e., the acceptance of spiritual rights among different ethnic groups and nations, and because the Shariah, who was aware of the future, did not express his displeasure with this practice, it should be accepted and considered valid. In addition to this, Imami jurists have argued for other documents such as the necessity of secondary titles, its acceptance in terms of government rulings, rational concentration and the inclusion of the authority of the guardian of jurisprudence.

Ayatollah Fazil Lankarani writes about this: Although Imam Khomeini has denied the Shariah validity of these rights, but it seems impossible that he would consider the rights that are intellectually recognized as right and impose effects on them, until there is a Shariah reason for denying the right. They are not established; they cannot be negated. Just as in the case of property, it is not necessary for evidence to prove it, but the absence of proof of non-property is enough to prove Shari'a as well as rationally. In the case of intellectual and spiritual rights, the logic is that they have been given value and credibility.

Today, in all the rational societies and legal systems of the world, this issue is part of the rights for which they value it and it is reserved for the right holder, so that no one other than him has the right to use it, and if someone uses this right without his permission, both from the point of view of custom, he has done a wrong and distasteful act and can be prosecuted from the point of view of punishment. Ayatollah Montazeri, in response to a question about intellectual works, considers that possession of them depends on the author's permission due to customary ownership. The text of his question and answer is as follows.

Question

CDs have been arranged and popularized that contain scientific and practical software in various fields of science, including the fields of beliefs, jurisprudence, interpretation and hadith, and for their use, locks have been used by their organizers and without it. Usually, it is difficult or impossible to use those CDs, but some people use special tricks to remove the said lock and reproduce them without the permission and consent of the organization that regulates them. Is this act legally permissible?

Answer

The mentioned site and CDs and their software such as patents and copyrights have customary property and any disturbance in the site or use of CDs by breaking their lock without the permission of the regulatory institution is forbidden in Sharia and causes violation of the rights of others and the guarantor. It is worth mentioning that some jurists, including ayatollah haeri, do not consider it to be a valid reason due to the lack of connection between intellectual property and intellectual property. In fact, Imam Khomeini should be considered one of those jurists who consider the validity of the life history to be dependent on its connection to the time of the Shariah in all cases, but as others have said, the validity of the life history is inherent and does not need the signature of the Shariah and connection to his time.

Supremacy rule

Invoking the rule rule is correct if it applies to rights and property. Some jurists consider property to be valid only for nobles and do not consider it to include rights, but as Imam Khomeini wrote: some rights are definitely considered as property. Because a price is paid in front of them and nothing else is valid in terms of taxation. Considering that intellectual rights are valuable.

Some jurists consider the possession of others to be subject to the owner's permission based on the rule of dominion. Ayatollah Hosseini Rouhani writes about this: Whoever composes something, that composition is the result of his intellectual work and thought, and therefore he owns it and has the right to prevent others from interfering in it. Because people are in control of their property according to law and custom. Of course, his ownership is not absolute, and there is no reason for the sanctity of usufruct and spiritual possessions, such as reading and citing it. What is not allowed is copying and reproduction without the author's permission, in which case he can claim the right.

The sanctity of seizing other people's property without their permission: one of the reasons for the legitimacy of intellectual property rights and the inadmissibility of seizing it without the creator's permission. Ayatollah Sanei wrote in response to a question about the reproduction of other people's works: It is forbidden and impermissible to reproduce other people's works, which are prohibited by them, and how can a valuable thing that traditionally belongs to others and is considered their property be taken over without obtaining the consent of their owners is permissible and there is no difference between the external object or benefit or effect.

Because all of them are financially related to others and valuable and added to them. Therefore, the permission to occupy in any form depends on the good nature and satisfaction of their owners. In response to a question about patent rights, the aforementioned person also writes: Everyone has the right and authority over his inventions and intellectual, scientific and experimental works, and taking possession of them is taking over another's right, which is forbidden and impermissible without his consent and permission.

Ayatollah Makarem Shirazi also writes about the ruling on intellectual property: Intellectual property is respected like material property, and trespassing on its privacy is not allowed, and anyone who trespasses and causes damage is a guarantor. Because ownership is one of the common and rational issues, and in other words, it is one of the issues that are determined by custom and reason, and we know that in our age and time, this type of ownership is recognized by custom and reason, and since the issue is determined by custom.

We take the ruling from Sharia. In addition, they spend millions and spend hundreds of hours to invent an industrial device or discover a medicine or write a book course or produce a CD. Heinous oppression has been committed and oppression is forbidden according to Sharia law and reason, and if those who commit this wrongdoing by illegal means, it is not proof that it is permissible and they are the guarantors.

Velayat-e-Faqih solution

Some jurists have accepted the legitimacy of intellectual property rights by citing the Velayat-e-Faqih solution. Ayatollah Ha'eri writes: Whenever a jurist sees the interest of the community in the necessity of gathering such rights, he uses his authority and establishes these rights. Therefore, if a jurist, for example, declares the publication of a personal authorship forbidden to the general public without his permission, the author can charge an amount from the publisher in exchange for the permission to publish his writing.

If his book is published without his permission, it is obligatory on the publisher to pay the price of the publishing rights to the author based on the basis of the jurisprudence. It is worth noting that the mentioned other arguments that have been established on the legitimacy of intellectual property rights are incomplete and he accepts only the solution of religious authority. Even though Ayatollah Safi

Golpayegani has not accepted the legitimacy of intellectual property rights, he holds the right to limit the use of these rights for a certain period of time.

Harmless rule

A person who writes a book, produces a movie or invents an invention may incur a lot of costs. If people are allowed to reproduce an intellectual work, screen a movie, or mass produce an invention, it will entail harm to the creators of such works, which should be prevented based on the rule of harmlessness. Although there is a difference of opinion in the interpretation of the no-harm rule, whether we take the said rule to mean the negation of a harmful sentence, the prohibition of damages, or the negation of unjustified harm, seizing such rights is not permissible and requires the permission of their owners.

Material of Mursalah

One of the sources of Islamic law in Sunni jurisprudence is the base of material of Mursalah. The purpose of transmission or correction is expedient thoughts that are in harmony with the possessions and intentions of the holy Sharia, but we have not received a specific reason from the side of religion for its cancellation or validity. Therefore, if a mujtahid finds the event, he needs in the Shari'ah, he takes refuge in the means of the message.

In applying the rule of the interests of the party to intellectual property rights, it can be said that there is an important public interest in protecting these rights, which belongs to all human societies, and that is the interest of intellectual values that have an effect in various aspects of life, and for this reason, including rights It is considered divine. Because its benefit is general and its position is great and the expediency of the message is observed in religion and the rulings are imposed on it. Because the expediency of the sender is one of the foundations of justice and truth. Therefore, intellectual phenomena are property.

It is worth noting that the above-mentioned rule is not a valid reason from the opinion of Imamiyyah jurists and some schools of Sunni jurisprudence because it is suspect.

Chapter IV

Punishment of intellectual property violators in Imami jurisprudence

Violation of intellectual property

Violation of intellectual property means that one of the material or intellectual rights resulting from intellectual property is used without their permission, which damages one of the material or intellectual rights created or transferred to any of the material rights belonging to that material and the loss comes.

According to this definition, if an individual's scientific, artistic and musical works are used without his permission or transmitted for reproduction, distribution or display in a public media, or a film that a film company has produced exclusively from a sports competition, without the permission of the holder of the right to broadcast on television or the Internet, or a book or a scientific article belonging to an author without his permission to be published or broadcast in a public media under another name or in a distorted form, the violation has been realized.

The following elements are required to realize the violation of the rights of creators in mass media according to the UK copyright law:

- ✓ To copy the creator's work.
- ✓ The copied work should be offered to the public.
- ✓ The work from which it is copied has already been presented to the public.
- ✓ Supplying the copied works to the public through their broadcast and publication in one of the public media.

Illegal competition

Any competition that is conducted against the honorable custom of industry or business is considered illegal competition. Clause 3 of Article 10 of the Paris Convention states and prohibits examples of illegal competition. According to this clause, the following actions should be specifically prohibited:

- ✓ Commercial competition by misrepresenting the institution or products or industrial activity.

- ✓ Specifications or statements that, by using it in commerce, will cause a general misunderstanding about the nature, construction, distinguishing features of the product, usability or quality of the product.
- ✓ Making false statements in business in a way that discredits the institution or the products or business of a competitor.

According to the above, the use of trade names, trademarks and packaging of third parties' products to introduce their products and offer them in the market is considered illegal competition. Because in these cases, a person intends to show his product similar to other people's product by using unrealistic titles.

For example, National is a well-known trademark for Matsushita Electric Company in Japan. If someone else creates a business called National Penlight using the National mark, this action can be called an instance of unfair competition. The exclusive rights of the owner of the trademark require that others are prohibited from any action that involves the violation or weakening of these rights or that misleads consumers and leads to unfair competition. There are conditions for such prohibited actions, i.e., unauthorized use of the mark, some of which are briefly as follows:

- ✓ The use of the mark is not based on registration.
- ✓ The sign should not be used in real terms.
- ✓ The use of the mark is not based on the consent of the right holder.
- ✓ The use of the mark is commercial.

Types of intellectual property violations

Actions that mislead consumers and cause the loss of the primary interests of the claimant, or cause a person to be deceived or positive about the authenticity of the goods and services, have been examined in the following statements.

Copyright violation on the Internet

In this case, the problem also occurs when the uploading of copyrighted materials occurs across borders. For example, there may be a claim that a person residing in France infringes a copyright in Germany without seeking permission from an English company. Because this lawsuit is related to three countries, similar questions arise. Which country's court has the right to judge this case, and what law should be applied in this case?

Types of copyright infringement

Copyright infringement is done by taking any unauthorized action in relation to the whole or an essential part of the protected work any copying, reproduction, publication, performance, distribution and broadcasting of a work subject to the protection of copyright laws, if done without the permission of the author or any other holder of said right, is considered a violation of the author's rights and causes liability. American courts consider the violation of the essential part of the work to be a violation of the copyright and consider the quality of the violation and not its quantity to be the fundamental rule of the violation.

Copyright infringement can be done in two ways

Primary violation: Primary violation is actually doing and implementing any of the author's exclusive rights without his permission. The exclusive rights of the author generally include: the right to reproduce, present and offer the work to the public, perform and broadcast it in various ways, including through radio and television. If a person performs one of these actions with respect to a literary or artistic work or software subject to protection, without the permission of the copyright holder, he has committed a primary violation.

In such cases where the author's rights are violated directly, the personal responsibility of the violator of said rights is absolute, and it is not necessary to prove the fault of the defendant, but it is sufficient to prove the damage caused and the relationship between the cause of the damage and the act of the defendant, and not even the defendant. He can escape responsibility by proving his innocence.

Secondary violation

Secondary violation of copyright is in a way that the said rights are not directly violated, but in some kind of context of violation such as importing, selling or distributing or any transaction regarding the infringed works subject to the copyright. is provided the important and common feature of this type of violation, which separates it from the basic violation, is the existence of the element of knowledge and awareness to realize the responsibility of the agent to compensate for the damage.

Of course, actual knowledge is not a condition, but the existence of any circumstances and circumstances that indicate the person's conventional knowledge and knowledge, in such a way that if a conventional person other than the defendant is placed in the place of the defendant in the aforementioned special circumstances, and the subject of the act infringing the rights of another author Be aware, it is enough.

Copyright problems on the Internet

The relationship between the Internet and copyright law is complex. The Internet is an international system for transferring and reproducing content, most of which are protected by copyright. However, it creates unimaginable possibilities for copyright infringement and challenges copyright law.

The following features of the Internet have created special problems for copyright law

- ❖ Information may be easily reproduced and distributed. That is, when the information is digitally on a computer connected to the Internet, that information can be easily uploaded, downloaded and distributed.
- ❖ Internet users expect free access to copyrighted material. In other words, most copyrighted materials published on the Internet are available for free. This has caused users to resist paying for internet content.
- ❖ Internet users may act anonymously. Therefore, it is difficult to determine the internet user individually. Therefore, users may commit copyright infringement with a low probability of detection, especially if the infringements are limited and not permanent.

Framing

Framing is another type of dynamic communication that is similar to an in-program communication link that allows the website designer to drag the entire external site into the program and design around it with their own framework. The effect of this is the same as an in-app affiliate link in that the external site appears to be part of the local site and the URL remains unchanged.

The communication link has two forms: the above-text communication link and the in-program communication link. The communication link with the reference above the text appears on the page with the highlighted phrase and is separated from the text with a special color or format an example is the underlined item. When an Internet user clicks on a communication link and activates it, the web browser software retrieves the corresponding text from the external site and creates a copy that is displayed on the screen any connection to the local site is simultaneously terminated when the searcher establishes a connection to the external site.

This type of communication is called an outbound communication link. If the user checks the URL on the browser, the URL will change from the user's start page to the link page. The risk of intra-program link is that the Internet users think that the communication sites are connected to each other. This risk increases when intra-program communication and framing are used.

As a result, users cannot recognize that the source of the content is an external site, and it is mistakenly considered the source of the information. In such cases, if many countries are involved in this type of litigation, the courts of all these countries may file a lawsuit regarding the judicial process.

If such cases occur in another country, will the court use the same law and judgment of the country of origin? Because different countries may have different exceptions to copyright, once jurisdiction is decided, the court will determine what law should apply.

Upload copyrighted materials

Because transferring copyrighted materials through the Internet is simple and common, many Internet users consider the fact of uploading copyrighted materials to their website. Because many uploading cases have occurred in America, there are three theories regarding copyright infringement under American law.

There are three theories of copyright infringement: direct infringement, vicarious infringement and vicarious infringement. The copyright act of 1976 deals with direct infringement. According to the 1976 law, infringement occurs when the infringer violates the copyright holder's exclusive rights, which include the right to reproduce, distribute, publicly display and perform the copyrighted work. Violation of aiding and abetting occurs when the offender knowingly, intentionally and knowingly contributes to the offending behavior of another.

In the same way, the vicarious violator is responsible for the various actions of the violator, when he has the ability to control and the right to restrain the violator's actions and obtains a direct financial advantage from the violation.

Download copyrighted materials

When copyrighted materials are uploaded and made available, Internet users download them in the next step. There is no doubt that users download such content without obtaining permission from the copyright holders. Copyright holders are also reluctant to file lawsuits against millions of infringers. On the other hand, a lot of attention has been paid to the responsibility of the parties who provide the equipment for illegal activities.

In the case of A.M. record company and his napster company, napster is able to transfer MPTR files. made it available to users and the company distributed its shared file software for free through its website and its users through the shared file process that is categorized in the central server, mp3 files. Downloaded these files were downloaded directly from the users' hard drive from the Internet. A.M. recorder and other related companies filed a copyright infringement lawsuit against napster in the United States district court in northern California.

The court believed that the Napster users who downloaded the files containing the copyright violated the plaintiff's reproduction rights. In fact, Napster was aware of the violation of the plaintiff's copyright by its users. In addition, without the provision of Napster support activities, users could not easily download music. This means that napster provided the site and facilities for direct violation and assisted in this work. In napster's vicarious infringement case, the district court noted that napster benefited financially from access to protected works on its system. Because the evidence showed that napster's future revenue depends on increasing the number of users. For this reason, the court determined that napster was able to monitor the rights policy and control access to the system. What should be said is that in these cases the following issues should be considered:

- ✓ Miran the power of the individual to prevent violations.
- ✓ The importance of the relationship between a person with authority and a person committing a violation.
- ✓ Has the person with legal authority taken legal steps to prevent the violation?

Violation of the rights of Internet addresses

Protection of Internet addresses to prevent the encroachment of others and the possible misuse of Internet addresses for profit-seeking purposes or misleading and obliviousness of consumers and in order to maintain possible order and create peace in a society orderly and civilized is absolutely necessary.

The holder or the legal owner of a name or internet address can use its priority or exclusive rights when he has registered it with the competent authorities. In some countries, such as Germany, France, America, Australia, the rule of priority is applied to establish the right of way.

Rights and privileges gain value when they are supported by domestic and international authorities. In the same way, infringement is realized when a person or persons register a similar address by unauthorized use of another Internet name and imitating its constituent elements. Although the latter assumption is almost impossible, but the impossible assumption is not impossible. Violation of rights caused by the name and Internet address may or may not be malicious, so in this context, 2 assumptions are conceivable:

In the first assumption, a person with knowledge and knowledge of the existence of the right of precedence in the field of Internet name belonging to a third party intentionally registers it in his own name or obligingly registers it for himself with misleading changes in the Internet address. In this case, trespassing with fraud and bad faith must have the necessary civil and criminal enforcement guarantee, so that the rights of the owners of priority rights are protected.

The second assumption is that the applicant registers a similar internet name or a different name and address without knowledge and knowledge of the existence of history. In this assumption, the action taken may be completely accidental and rare, in which case no damage should be done to the right holder, and such infringements should be eliminated through the cancellation of the next registered name, and the damage caused to the owner of the priority right should also be done. be compensated in addition, the registering authority should be held responsible for such damages due to the fault caused by the lack of accuracy.

Although, due to the absence of malicious intent, the guarantee of criminal enforcement of such actions is excluded, but the claimant will have the right to refer to the registry to receive compensation from the victim according to the legal rule of harmlessness from the domain name registrar.

Another important domain of intellectual property rights is the rights of trademark owners and industrial property in the electronic space. In the definition of a trademark, it is said that it is any word, name, sign, design or letter that is used in the business world to determine the identity of a specific product and distinguish it from other products. A trademark identifies the connection of a specific product with a specific company as the main source of production of that product. A trademark is a sign that distinguishes the goods produced or services provided by a person or an economic enterprise from the goods or services of another person or economic enterprise, and the consumer can distinguish the goods from other similar products by means of that mark.

A registered trademark creates a type of exclusive rights for its holder to use the said mark for the goods or services in question in the country where the mark is registered. In order to protect the rights of consumers and encourage legitimate competition in the context of electronic exchanges, the use of trademarks in the form of domains or any type of display on the line that can deceive a person about the authenticity of goods or services should also be supported in cyberspace. countries to be placed. The reason for this issue comes from the fact that companies, both small and large, often communicate with their customers by creating internet stations.

Infringing use of the name and trademark

The only reason why a non-claimant would want to use a domain name to include his trademark is if he wants to position himself or his product as a member of the claimant's class. Therefore, the use of these names and signs is considered to be the exclusive right of the claimants.

Trademark disputes occur globally on the Internet. Therefore, there is a possibility of a potential violation of the claimants' trademark rights. Therefore, claimants in different countries can proceed on the basis that trademark infringement occurred there. In such a situation, the courts of these countries apply judicial procedures on the issues of violation of common ownership and make various decisions according to their laws.

Using another brand name as the domain name of the brand name law

One of the new phenomena related to cyber-crimes, which is also the basis of civil liability, is a phenomenon called cyber scouting. Cyber-scouting means that a person registers a domain name in his own name using the names and trademarks of other people, so that later, in suitable situations, he can sell the said domain name to the same persons who own the said trademarks at the price he wants.

The term Top Level Domain (TLD) refers to the general description, dotcom, dotnet, etc., or it indicates the country where the domain name is registered. When a website is created for business purposes, Internet users expect SLD. (second level domain) contain the desired company name or brand name. Domain names not only serve as users' Internet addresses, but also determine the ownership of their websites, products, or services.

However, any domain name can designate a site and is globally unique, although the territorial scope and nature of the brand name makes it possible for several companies to use the same brand name, for example, Panda. Therefore, there are situations called concurrent use where both parties feel they have the right to use the domain name for their own company or brand name. There is another type of situation called internet title registration or domain name theft, where the infringer registers a trademark as a domain name with the aim of profiting from it by selling it to the trademark owner.

The Internet Association for Assigned Names and Numbers is a non-profit association that is responsible for determining IP addresses, allocating Internet space, determining protocol parameters, domain names, and system management in order to guarantee the uniqueness of the identity of names on the Internet.

Use of another brand name in the content of the website

The territorial brand law makes it possible for different merchants to use the same brand name for services or goods under different judicial procedures. However, the Internet is global in nature and does not know territorial boundaries, and the content posted on the website is available all over the world. Therefore, the marks or trade names placed by the merchant on the Internet carry the risk of violating the trade names registered in other legal proceedings.

Courts in different countries may adopt a different approach. Although neither the parties nor the brand are related to each other, they may enforce the law based on the fact that the infringing website is globally accessible and that there is a locus of infringement and a locus of law enforcement. The result is that the courts of different countries apply the law on the same case and make different decisions. Trademark infringement is when a person actively pursues a commercial activity in the relevant country. In addition, if the infringer who includes the brand name on the website pursues his business activity and profit in several countries or at the global level, the case will be related to these countries and their brand laws will be used to determine the case. are implemented.

To explain the issues, we assume that the case is related to two different countries. First, if one country has a similar approach to the use of a brand name on the Internet, and another country considers the brand name to be universal and usable everywhere as soon as it is placed on the Internet, the application of the laws of these two countries will lead to completely different results. done Second, if two countries have the same test and benchmark for using a brand name on the Internet, their courts will make different decisions based on different standards for determining the extent of commercial activities according to their brand laws. Therefore, the use of another brand name on the website involves legal action.

Use of another brand name as the main label

Another issue regarding the expansion of the Internet is whether the use of the main label of a word that is similar to another brand name is an infringement of that brand name or whether is not?

The nature of the main sticker

A main sticker is a word that is written on a web page in an electronic language such as HTML. is written When such a tag is inserted on a web page, it is not easily visible to Internet users, but Internet search engines notice its invisible presence. Search engines use keywords to determine and rank web pages appropriately.

As there are clear benefits to being close to search results, tags are considered an important feature in web page marketing. Many website owners use original tags that include common terms such as law and lawyer. As no person has a legal right to such terms, there is no legal claim over it. This lawsuit arises when website owners use their competitors' trademarks as their primary tags.

Selling the brand name as a keyword

The recent growth in the brand name related to the Internet is related to the sale of the brand name as a keyword. In response to a site search, search engines search sites to find the terms entered in the search box.

The words that the internet user types in the box are called keywords. Therefore, when the website owner is not satisfied with his position in the search engine results, despite the fact that he has used generic terms or competitors' brand names in the main tag, he has another way to pay the search engines, so that whenever the Internet user Enter the words and his website will appear.

When the sale of keywords only includes general words, there is no legal claim and no one has a legal right to these general terms, but when the keyword being sold is a brand name, a violation statement is entered. Due to the global nature of keywords, a plaintiff can pursue an infringement case in many countries. Because there are international disputes about the issue of selling a brand name as a keyword, it seems that courts in different countries make different decisions about a keyword case after determining the jurisdiction. The main question in these types of cases is whether the infringing activities include taking advantage of the brand name or not? For example, in the case of Rescue Com and Google, the United States District Court in the Northern District of America stated that Rescue Com could not prove that the sale of the trademark by Google as a keyword constitutes exploitation of the trademark.

Therefore, Google's actions are not considered trademark infringement. In this case, the purchase and sale of the brand name as a keyword was not considered as profit from the brand name, but such an approach is not the same and several American local courts have reached different conclusions about this debate. For example, in the case of Edina Realty and M.L.S. online.com A district court in Minnesota ruled that the infringer's commercial purchase of the plaintiff's trademark as a keyword constituted commercial use. On the contrary, in the case of two companies, Merck and Co. and Mediplan Health Consulting, the United States District Court in the Southern District of New York stated that the profitable purchase of the plaintiff's brand name as a keyword is a type of internal use and is not a profitable use of the brand name. Because the infringers do not include the plaintiff's mark on any of the goods and do not use them to indicate the sponsor or source.

Therefore, the courts cannot agree whether the sale of the trademark in the form of keyword advertising is considered to be the use of the trademark or not? Courts of different countries may adopt different approaches to this issue. Although neither the parties nor the brand are related to each other, they may enforce the law based on the fact that the infringing website is globally accessible and that there is a locus of infringement and a locus of law enforcement. The consequence of such a problem is that the courts of different countries apply the law to a similar case and make different decisions.

Patent violation

According to the definition of the World Intellectual Property Organization, an invention is a product or process that provides a new way to do something or proposes a new technical solution to solve a specific problem. A license or patent certificate is granted by the requested government or country to the inventor or his legal representative. The holder of the copyright certificate has an exclusive right to exploit the patented invention.

Monopoly is a set of unique rights that are given to a specific person by the government for a certain period of time. With the expiration of the patent protection period, the patent protection will end and its use will be available to the public. In fact, what is protected as an invention in the network are commercial methods, and this is not accepted in many countries.

On the other hand, establishing less protections and leaving open ways for the possibility of more use in the legal systems of developing and less developed countries requires reducing the protected cases. Finally, although one cannot deny the acceptance of invention in digital technology, if we want to consider some things as inventions in the scene of communication and information exchange, we will face many problems.

In fact, a difference should be made between two discussions, one is technology and the other is the activity and relationships of persons in the said environment. The topic of the present research is related to the activities and topics in general in the virtual space.

Patent business methods

Courts have not issued many guidelines in the application of substantive rights regarding infringement cases related to patent business methods. For example, in the case of Amazon.com and Barnes and Noble.com, the United States District Court in the Western District of Washington briefly compared Amazon's patent, which was guided by the one-click method and Internet shopping order system, with

Barnes and Noble's one-click verification system and According to his final decision, Amazon's patent was infringed.
The district court affirmed the preliminary injunction grant analysis, but the appellate court reversed the preliminary injunction, finding that Barnesandnoble had raised a substantial issue of the validity of Amazon's patent. Then the case was settled and no further follow-up was done.
Although this case was resolved, due to the borderless nature of the Internet, potential issues can be raised in such cases. This means that the courts of these countries first decide and litigate the legal jurisdiction, and after deciding on this matter, it is determined what law should be applied.

Software patent

The court has issued few guidelines regarding the enforcement of substantive rights in infringement cases regarding this type of patent. For example, in Iolas Technologies and Microsoft Corporation, the United States District Court for the Northern District of Illinois did not do much analysis of Iolas' patent infringement in Internet search software, but followed the jury's findings on infringement and ruled on that basis.
When Microsoft appealed, the Court of Appeals emphasized the issue of re-evaluating new judgment cases and the case was settled. Now, if the parties in this case are from different countries, or the infringed product is sold on the Internet to people in different countries, the case will be related to several countries. In such a situation, patent infringement action requires rethinking the legal field and choosing legal issues. Internet infringement has caused many problems for Internet intellectual property law. To face these issues, digital technologies have been used to protect the rights of property infringement, which we will examine in the next section.

The development of Internet technology as a way to prevent intellectual property violations:

Individuals and companies sometimes use technical tools to protect their intellectual property rights. Today's Internet technology is facing many problems and there are many obstacles in the way of the development of the current system, which we will examine below.

Technical tools to ensure the rights of the owners of the works: these tools include serial copy management system, coding, digital signature and finally watermarking, which we will review below.

SCMS (Serial Copy Management System)

SCMS It was introduced by companies that make it possible to create original copies of sounds on digital audio tapes. SCMS, it uses a copy control banner that is embedded in the content and verifies whether copying is allowed or not. In original products that are subject to copy protection, the copy bit is always on. On copy-free discs where no copy right restrictions apply, the copy bit is always off. In this system, if the user tries to make a copy from the copy tool, the serial copy management system rejects the command. The disadvantage of this system is that software and design defects in certain models of the client's mini disc player may cause the SCM to fail.

Coding: The purpose of coding is to prevent unauthorized copying by masking the contents, so that they cannot be accessed. If the contents are effectively encrypted, the files cannot be easily copied. Because it is not possible to access the contents without a password. A widely used cryptosystem is the public key system.

This system requires two special keys: public key and private key. These two keys are associated with the receiver to which the data is sent. The public key is distributed across the interface, while the private key is kept secret by the receiver. Data updated using a person's public key can be decrypted using that person's private key. By applying this technology to individual property rights and protecting it, the copyright holder can encode a work using the intended receiver's public key. After the owner sends the encrypted work, the receiver uses his private key to decrypt it, and other parties cannot decrypt or read it.

The advantage of using this technology is that it makes it possible to limit access to the work and allocate it to royalty payers, and it reduces the amount of internet content theft and quick access and makes it undetectable. If the encryption is not strong enough, mathematical technology can be used to decrypt the work without the need for a key, or if the key distribution protocol is flawed, an unauthorized person may obtain the code through advanced technology or social engineering and surveillance.

Digital signatures: In addition to encryption, another application is digital signature encryption. Digital signature schemes include a pair of cryptographic keys that must be generated for the sender. The sender keeps the private key, but releases the public key. To sign some data, the sender uses a special software to calculate and evaluate the data, such as its contents and characteristics, which is known as the mixing function. He encrypts this abstract with a private key to create a digital signature. When the receiver receives the data and the digital signature, it uses the sender's public key to decrypt the digital signature.

He then creates a combination of data using the combination function and compares both. If they are exactly the same, the receiver knows that the data was not tampered with after signing and was sent using the sender's private key. However, there are some problems that digital signature cannot solve. For example, the data may be accessible from some other paths as well, such as falsification of the encryption program or loading by the user.

Watermarking: Another technology is digital watermarking. Watermarking allows copyright holders to include invisible information in their works to determine the originality of the content. Digital watermarks are bits that are included in the content and can be read by a detection tool, and with its help, it is possible to understand whether the content is authentic or not and where the content originates from. Watermarking's can contain information about the author's name and email address, as well as information about who owns the work, how to contact the owner of the work, and whether or not a price must be paid to use the work. The most common use of watermarking is to paste the copyright statement on the work. One of the problems of watermarking is that it must remain under file compression methods and cannot be seen or heard when the file is decompressed.

Violation of intellectual property in Imami jurisprudence

Applying the rule of waste to the violation of intellectual rights: according to the rule of waste in jurisprudence, whoever wastes another's property is its guarantor, and according to the opinions of jurists, the knowledge and intention of the waste have no effect on his guarantee. In spite of the fact that some jurists believe that this rule is valid, according to the opinion of the majority of them, it seems that the rule of wastage is arbitrary.

Based on this, examining the vocabulary of the rule will be effective in explaining it. Loss from the material "waste" means to be destroyed and destroyed. The idiomatic meaning of atalaf is used in the words of jurists, including atalaf in the literal sense. Therefore, in jurisprudential terminology, eating is considered a waste, but the scholars do not call it waste.

Because eating is not wasting food. Loss in the language of jurists has two types: real and legal. Real waste means that a person destroys the same property of another person, in such a way that it can no longer be used and used, such as burning clothes, destroying a house, but in a decreed waste, the property itself exists and is not destroyed, but its value and property. It is destroyed, like if one or more ice cubes are usurped from someone in the summer and the same one is handed over to him the next year in the winter, which in this case remains the same property, but its value has been lost. There is no doubt about the inclusion of the rule in relation to actual loss, but the jurists have differed regarding the legal loss.

A large number of jurists have considered the rule of waste to be special to real waste, and they have not considered waste of judgment within the rule, and they believe that the loss of property mentioned in the text of the rule is waste, which is the subject of the consensus of jurists, or the subject of the rule is the same as true waste.

Therefore, in the case where the property is lost, but the original property remains, the guarantee cannot be based on this rule. Some other jurists, while rejecting this argument, believe that despite the lack of legal destruction of property, the deterioration of the price can be considered as legal and virtual loss. The late Imam Khomeini also developed the same argument and considers the rule of waste to include the cases of ordered waste. The latter view seems reasonable. Because the purpose of establishing the rule of loss is to compensate the loss that has been inflicted on the owner of the property, and in the case of liquidated damages, the loss is realized. Violation of intellectual rights, according to its definition, seems to be a waste of judgment.

Because without the principle of the intellectual right being lost and destroyed, the right holder's sovereignty over the intellectual right is lost and at least he suffers a loss in relation to the benefits obtained from the infringed part. It may be claimed that in some cases, such as the use of a sculpture, its exploitation can be associated with the deterioration of the original work in the form of actual loss. For example, a person uses a sculpture until it is destroyed.

In this case, the use of the statue is apparently associated with its actual decay and destruction. In response, it can be said that under no circumstances and in any case of intellectual property rights can it be assumed that actual loss has occurred, in such a way that it can be prosecuted by referring to the provisions of intellectual property rights. For example, in the case that a person without the permission of the sculptor uses the statue designed by him in his film and the statue falls and disintegrates during filming, it cannot be claimed that the disintegration of the statue is a violation of intellectual rights.

Violation of intellectual rights here is the unauthorized use of the sculpture in the film. Violation of intellectual rights cannot lead to actual damages in any way due to the violation of intellectual rights. Because its principle is always immaterial. This is why some jurists have used the interpretation of mental objects to describe these rights.

The coordinates of what is called wealth are: the ability to acquire and allocate, being needed, people's desire for it and the willingness to pay in exchange for receiving it, economic value, stopping its acquisition on effort and its customary validity. Contrary to Western law, which in modern times has acknowledged the property of immaterial objects, there has always been such an approach in Islamic jurisprudence that the acceptance of the concept of general property in the fiqh is the main evidence of this claim. This is because there is a difference between object and property in Islamic law.

Affirming that the interests of objects and actions of persons are property is also based on this approach in Islamic law. The acceptance of the ownership of some examples of property in the current era, such as data and information, has long been a precedent in Islamic jurisprudence, and even some jurists, in order to dispel any doubt in this field, have explicitly stated that the same externality or material and tangible embodiment is a condition It is not belonging. Intellectual property seems to have all these coordinates and the jurists in favor of ownership of intellectual rights, including in some cases, referring to the economic value of such rights in custom and constructive ownership, have considered ownership and ownership to be fixed. There is no doubt that people feel the need for technology and innovation in intellectual property and are willing to pay for it.

In addition, the assignment of the patent to the inventor or the author's right to the creation is due to the act that the inventor has done and according to the many verses and traditions that consider the establishment of private ownership dependent on human efforts. In addition, data and information have been considered property in

Imami jurisprudence for a long time. Some foreign researchers also explicitly consider the subject of intellectual property rights to be data and information. Data and information that is valuable and people are willing to pay money to get that information.

Currently, according to the laws and regulations of taxation, the subjects and belongings of intellectual property rights are recognized and valid. The mere use of this credit is enough to confirm the ownership of intellectual rights. It is based on this credit that in article 1 of the Law on Encouragement and Support of Foreign Investment approved in 1380, under the heading of examples of foreign capital that can be attracted and supported, along with property such as machinery, equipment, etc., patents, technical know-how, names and signs Commercial and specialized services have also been specified.

Now, this issue can be raised whether it is possible to apply the rule of loss to intellectual property that is not tangible? The owner of the jewelry considers loss as a guarantee, whether the subject is the same, such as a torn garment, or benefit, such as living in a house. Shahid Sani also considers the usurper's guarantee for the interests of the usurper's property to be correct in the book of usurpation. Also, Allama Hali and Mohaghegh Sani also specify the guarantee of benefits. On this basis, if the subject of intellectual property rights is considered an immaterial object, it is considered as an immaterial object and is subject to management in waste.

If it is considered a credit matter that has benefits, it will be subject to loss of benefits. According to some jurists, the reason for the guarantee of benefits is the same as the reason for the guarantee of the object. Because the benefit guarantee is the effect and requirement of the same guarantee, and in this regard, there is no difference between the interests of beneficiaries and non-beneficiaries. On the other hand, some jurists such as Shahid Sani, Shahid Aul and Fazel Moqdad have considered stopping in this field. This is explained that because they were faced with the reasons for both proving the guarantee and not proving the guarantee of non-mustufat interests and they did not find a preference for one, they seized it and did not issue a fatwa. Some other jurists have not easily accepted the inclusion of guarantee for the benefits of the non-mustufat.

In this context, Sheikh Ansari believes that there is a reason for both guarantee and non-guarantee in this case. Loss of purpose and loss of benefit are both signs of the rule of loss, and based on that, it is possible to decide on the compensation of damages for loss of purpose or benefit.

In other words, even if we do not consider intellectual rights to be the same thing and consider it as the benefit and result of human work, there is still no doubt about it including the rule of waste. However, it may be objected that the rule of loss includes only current and existing benefits and does not include future benefits, and since the benefit is not derived from existing intellectual property, then its violation will not be subject to the rule of loss. In jurisprudence, although some people do not believe in guaranteeing the interests of free people, some have accepted the guarantee of interests based on the rule of Ali Al-eed. Sahib Javaher's words are clear in this context and he considered the act of a free man to have financial value even before exchange and actualization. In violation of intellectual rights, the flow of the rule of loss is not hindered.

The provisions of intellectual rights are information and they are valuable, and if they are used without permission, it can be said that the user has wasted them. This analysis doubted the case where intellectual property entered the commercial markets and was welcomed by the public, such as an invention that has a buyer in the market or a book that was published and the public did not enter the market, for example, an invention or a book.

Because here, apparently, the property of intellectual property does not have economic value to be subject to the rule of loss. On the other hand, it can be said that if, along with Mirza Rashti, we consider only information as property, the information contained in intellectual property is also considered property, and as a result, its violation will be responsible.

If this analysis is not accepted and considering the special nature of intellectual rights, it will be difficult and even impossible to simply refer to the rule of loss in order to pay compensation to the owner of the intellectual right as a result of the violation of his right. Therefore, although considering the property of intellectual rights, including the rule of loss, there can be no serious doubts about it, but unlike material property, simply relying on this rule in the assumption of violation of intellectual rights does not necessarily lead to a breach of warranty, and as a result, the owner of the right has a problem.

Criticism of the flow of the rule of loss on the violation of intellectual rights
According to the definition of the violation of intellectual rights, it seems like a legal loss. Also in the place where due to the lack of commercialization of the subject of the intellectual right, it is not possible to consider the loss of benefits or harm to the owner of the right, and also in cases where the violation of the right not only did not cause damage to the owner, but also resulted in benefits for him, such as the assumption when a highly rejected and abandoned book is published illegally and causes the fame of its author, it is possible to rule on the flow of the rule of waste by referring to the wealth of information in jurisprudence. The realization of the title of waste in relation to the violation of intellectual property rights has been mentioned by some authors citing legal and jurisprudential evidence.
Based on the application of the property title to intellectual property including inventions, the exclusivity of these properties, and the validity of the title of loss to all properties such as real and potential interests and interests, they have accepted the realization of the title of loss to infringement of intellectual property, including inventions is the time of development of intellectual property rights varies depending on the case? Patent and trademark rights are not realized unless they are registered in the competent authority according to the regulations.
On the other hand, the time of development of the right of intellectual property to literary and artistic work is the moment when the original work is expressed by the creator in the form of media such as books, articles, films, audio works, etc. The primary and specific purpose of industrial property rights is to provide public benefits, but the copyright system primarily provides the protection of the personal

rights of creators, and thus public rights are also fulfilled. Now the issue is, does the mere violation of intellectual property rights cause a loss of profit?

According to the provided definition of infringement as soon as a patent or trademark is registered or a book is authored, if someone uses the said invention or registered trademark or prints the book in question, it is an intellectual right violation has been realized and as a result the right holder is entitled to receive damages, but in practice it does not seem to be the case. Because the rule of loss is one of the foundations of civil responsibility in Iranian jurisprudence and law, but it does not destroy the pillars of responsibility.

Therefore, if a patent is infringed, but the owner of the right cannot prove the damage caused to him or basically no immediate damage is caused, the order to compensate the damage will also be rejected. This is especially true for inventions that are merely patented, but have not yet entered the commercialization cycle. The same analysis is valid for a registered trademark that the owner of the trademark does not use in the commercial market.

If a person has registered a trademark, but does not market any product or service with it, although the use of that trademark by another person fulfills the concept of infringement, this action does not require damage to the owner of the trademark. In copyright, there may be cases where, despite the violation, the owner of the right does not suffer or even benefits.

For example, a person may express his literary taste behind the closed doors of his room in the form of poems and express it in his manuscripts without any intention other than to convince his literary aesthetic sense. There is no doubt that these manuscripts are known and can be protected according to the law, assuming the existence of the original work, although the poet did not turn it into a poetry court to be sold in the market, nor does he even intend to do so.

Therefore, if someone else accesses these manuscripts and publishes them without obtaining permission from the poet, not only the claim of harm to the poet is not acceptable, but here it must be acknowledged that the infringement of the work has also caused the poet to profit. Therefore, in such cases, the owner of the invention, trademark or literary and artistic work will be deprived of compensation, and merely referring to the rule of loss cannot pave the way for receiving the right. In contrast to material properties, in which the mere reference to the waste rule does not face any moral or legal obstacles, the mere reference to the waste rule seems to be problematic in the violation of intellectual rights.

For example, the residence of an innocent wanderer in an abandoned house outside the city cannot be a positive right of the owner of the house to claim compensation based on the loss of benefits. Because such a house is not habitable in custom, and asking for a change in exchange for living in it is more like asking for no benefits than possible benefits.

According to the regulations, non-profit cannot be claimed. This sentence seems completely logical and compatible with justice and fairness, but in a similar case, i.e., the assumption that someone infringes the invention or book or trademark belonging to another, while his work has not entered the commercial market, if the sentence is If the compensation is not due to the owner of the intellectual right, there should be no doubt in its opposition to justice, fairness and the fundamentals of intellectual property rights. Intellectual property rights have certain foundations that distinguish them from traditional property.

Although the motivational role of this system may not have been explicitly considered in Iran's legal system, at least it can be claimed that this role is performed by the intellectuals of the society and its existence and importance have been unwritten.

For example, in the explanatory introduction of the 2013 Intellectual property protection bill, effective protection of intellectual property rights holders in the domestic and international arena and adapting the existing regulations to the needs of the world are among the reasons for presenting the said bill. Simply referring to the rule of loss, especially when the loss is attribution, is not an effective and sufficient method to protect the owners of intellectual rights, and if we also consider the establishment of fault in attribution as a condition of liability, the sufferings of the rights holder will be doubled. Because even in the assumption that intellectual property is commercialized, compensation will be excluded unless the infringer's fault is proven. Tasbib in Iranian jurisprudence and law is in the opposite sense of stewardship, that is, indirectly causing the loss of another's property.

According to some authors, loss means the loss of property without direct involvement. Some others consider destruction to mean the destruction of an object both in terms of creation and in terms of property, and in short, any transformation of an object in such a way that the custom of destruction is true for it, and even in the case of the survival of the object and the loss of its attributes and effects, referring to the validity of the loss of the wealth of the property has been considered fulfilled by Aqla. Some have considered things like drowning and theft as a waste if there is no possibility of finding it.

Therefore, in the assumption of loss through attribution, just like in general loss, something is always lost, which is property or human body, depending on the case. According to the above content, the question is raised, what is lost with the violation of intellectual rights? What we know is that due to the special nature of intellectual property, the truth of the title of loss regarding these properties cannot be easily accepted.

On the face of it, the violation of intellectual rights does not directly cause the loss of anything, as in the assumption of total loss of non-realized property. Because the violation of the intellectual right does not cause the destruction of the intellectual right itself, nor does it change its attributes and complications, but only causes the right holder to be deprived of some possible benefits.

Therefore, the violation of intellectual rights, whether it is called loss or compensation, is not the source of the effect from the point of view of compensation, except that the owner of the right will face more difficulties in the assumption of relying on the rule of compensation for damages. In the American legal system, attention has been paid to the fact that intellectual property rights are valuable in themselves and effective protection is provided.

On this basis, according to the special nature of intellectual rights in the American intellectual property rights system, there is an institution called legal damages, whereby the claimant in a copyright infringement lawsuit can claim legal damages instead of claiming actual damages, which requires accurate proof. claim, but contrary to the copyright system, such damages have been specified under the same title. In this legal system, regardless of the number of actual damages caused to it, which is calculated based on the criterion of lost benefits, it is considered a valuable asset, and in any case, if it is violated, a certain minimum economic value is considered to be compensated for it. Therefore, even if an invention has not been commercialized in practice that has a market benefit, or on the assumption of commercialization, the patent owner cannot prove the number of damages based on the criterion of lost benefits in the assumption of infringement, the court, relying on the conventional royalty criterion, he will calculate the number of damages and order to pay them. In the case of trademark infringement, the American trademark protection law, known as Lanham, considers the assumption that a person's trademark is counterfeited to be subject to legal damages.

One of the basic conditions of the claimant's entitlement in this assumption is the commercial use of the mark by the owner. Otherwise, the order to compensate the damages in favor of the plaintiff will depend on the proof of actual damages. It can be seen that if intellectual property rights are recognized in the American legal system, other regulations are also formed in line with this and there is no contradiction in this field, but in Iranian law, despite the explicit or implicit recognition of intellectual rights property, other provisions It is possible that it is contrary to this and their effect is rejected.

Relying on the rule of loss, at least in some cases, will deprive the owner of the right from claiming damages, and this is corrupt with the motivational role of this system, which may be questioned in Iran's legal system and is considered lacking in legal and jurisprudential foundations.

It seems that the prediction of such damages is supported by both jurisprudence and law. If according to some jurisprudential opinions, data and information have value and are subject to warranty, what is wrong with predicting the minimum number of damages in the assumption that due to the special nature of this information and

data, it is not possible to prove the actual number of damages for the right holder or it's hard. In this case, it is evident that the owner of the right has been damaged, but it is not possible to prove these damages or it is extremely difficult.
However, it may be claimed that there are rules in Iranian jurisprudence and law that can play a role in the same way as the institutions of legal damages and conventional royalties in America and provide appropriate means of compensation to the right holder in some cases. Some researchers have mentioned the institution of exemplary remuneration as a similar establishment in this field and have recommended its use while comparing it with conventional royalties in American law. Some people have been looking for a basis for compensation for the damages of the right holder in the event of violation of intellectual property rights by referring to the rule of unjust ownership or unjustified appropriation.

The rule of unjust possession in Iranian jurisprudence and law

Several verses in the Holy Quran prohibit unjust possession. Iranian law does not have a general and explicit rule regarding the prohibition of unjust possession, but this rule is the basis of many articles of the civil law, which shows the attention of the Iranian legislator to the importance of prohibiting unjust possession.

In article 307 of the Civil Code, the legislator has enumerated the causes of compulsory guarantee:

- ✓ Usurpation and what is usurpation.
- ✓ waste
- ✓ glorification
- ✓ Stifa

In this article, the rule of unjust possession is not mentioned. Taking a quick look at the articles of Iran's civil law, it becomes clear that Iran's legislator has established special institutions as much as possible by using Islamic jurisprudence and French law in order to prevent unjust acquisition.

Among other things, in article 387 of the civil law, considering that the customer did not receive anything in the valuable that he gave, the loss of the goods before the invoice was considered as the reason for the cancellation of the sale and the return of the price to the customer, and the seller is obliged to return the price in terms of unfair possession.

Also, in articles 390 to 393 of the civil code, in the case of the transfer of the goods to the third party, because the goods have not been transferred to the customer, the lawgiver ordered the return of the price to the customer, and the reason for the order is that the payment of the price to the seller is unreasonable and unfair. Acquiring non-eligible assets depends on the fulfillment of certain conditions, some of which are:

- ✓ Owning a person as a result of receiving financial or spiritual benefit.
- ✓ Decreasing the other party's property is due to the decrease in property and the loss of property, financial value, work, or the creation of undue expenses that are associated with the increase of another property.
- ✓ The causal relationship between the increase and decrease of assets.
- ✓ Lack of legal reason or contractual permission.

Therefore, whenever wealth is acquired through legal means, it is legitimate, and otherwise, the acquired property lacks a legitimate reason and is classified as illegitimate property.

Applying the rule regarding the violation of intellectual rights

Intellectual property rights have a special nature and function that distinguishes them from other properties. Titles such as right, property and property have different meanings in relation to intellectual phenomena and leave special effects. For example, regarding material property, when someone steals another car, the owner is deprived of the valuable property that he paid for it, while the thief does not pay for it.

That is, the thief gets free benefit from another's capital without paying any cost an apparently similar situation can also be imagined regarding intellectual property.

For example, when a person uses a story, creative product, or other trademark without permission, while this property was created with financial and time costs and risk assumption by the owner of the intellectual property, he violates the intellectual right without paying for the property.

The other will benefit for free. On the face of it, these two situations are the same, but further reflection shows that they are not. A car thief deprives its owner of his property, but the act of violating the intellectual right does not leave such an effect. Because the owner of the intellectual right is still free to use his property and, for example, he can transfer its use to another person through an exploitation license agreement.

In addition, although the violation of intellectual property may reduce the income of the right holder due to the deterioration of his exclusive right to use the intellectual property, this reduction will not be significant and may not even occur fundamentally. For example, the alleged infringement can involve the use of another's intellectual property for personal and non-commercial use. In this case, it is obvious that there is no decrease in the property of the right holder. Therefore, firstly, the unauthorized use of intellectual property does not break the relationship and interest between it and the owner of the property, and secondly, in some cases, it may not fundamentally reduce his property.

Violation of intellectual rights can be divided into several categories in terms of profit and loss for the infringer and the right holder:

- The infringer benefits from the act of infringement and at the same time the owner of the right suffers a loss.
- The infringer benefits from the act of infringement, but the owner of the right is not harmed.
- The infringer does not benefit from the act of violation and the owner of the right is harmed.
- The infringer does not benefit from the act of infringement and the right holder does not suffer any loss.

- The infringer does not benefit from the act of infringement and the right holder benefits from it in some way.

It is obvious that wherever a loss has occurred to the owner of the right, he can demand compensation for his loss by referring to the relevant provisions, including the civil liability law and the specific provisions of intellectual property rights. In this case, it does not make a difference whether the violator has also benefited from the violation of the right or not?

But where the loss to the owner of the intellectual right is not certain, such as the assumption that the inventor simply registered his invention, without commercializing it, is it possible to claim compensation for the damage by referring to the rule of unfair possession of the right? Intellectual property owner gave? If, in these cases, the infringer benefits and at the same time the property of the owner of the right is reduced, and the causal relationship between this increase and decrease is proven, there is no doubt that a verdict can be given to restore the benefits obtained against the infringer, but it seems that in there are several problems here. First, as it was said, intellectual rights have a special nature and their use without permission does not necessarily mean a reduction of property, especially in the case of the discussed assumption that the owner of the invention has only taken the initiative to register it in the offices of the Patent Office.

Secondly, in some cases, the violation of the right may not only cause loss to the owner, but also may not result in profit for the violator. For example, in this case, if the infringer produces products after using another invention to market, but before entering the market, all the products are destroyed due to a fire in the storage warehouse, despite the violation of the patent, the infringer's profit accrues. has not been therefore, the owner of the right cannot benefit from the guarantee of patent infringement executions provided in the patent law. Because according to article 181 of the executive regulations of the patent law regarding damages that are claimed either through legal channels or through criminal channels in lawsuits related to patents, industrial designs, marks and trade names, the damages will include the losses incurred.

Therefore, it can be said that applying the rule of unjust possession to compensate the intellectual rights owners is not possible and will not necessarily lead to compensation from them.

Examining moral damage compensation in jurisprudence

Regarding the position of spiritual damages in the Holy Qur'an, we can refer to some verses that prohibit both material and spiritual damages. Of course, in some verses, the issue of spiritual damage has been strongly dealt with. In our jurisprudential traditions, this issue has been discussed in detail. The issue of spiritual damages has been studied and researched in other jurisprudence books and has been discussed in the books of Islamic and Shia jurisprudence scholars.

Harmless rule

As mentioned, the harmless rule in Islamic law was first proposed by the Prophet of Islam, which was discussed in detail by Shia jurists, and it can be said that the main purpose of the legislation of this important rule It is the compensation for the damage caused to people, which in this narration is important and desirable for those spiritual damages.

As much as it is mentioned in our jurisprudence and historical books. According to Islamic historians, material damage was not meant in this story, but the Prophet of Islam issued an order in order to prevent one person from encroaching on another person's family privacy, which is referred to as the Harmful Rule in our jurisprudence.

Ways of compensation for moral damages

In fact, ways of compensation for moral damages are not very common and common compared to ways of compensation for material damages. What is certain is that the return of the same property, like or its price, is one of the methods of compensation for material damages, but in the matter of compensation for moral damages, such a thing is not envisaged.

For this reason, the methods of compensation for moral damage are limited and insufficient and somewhat unclear. Some jurists believe that no reliable means can be found to compensate for moral damage.

Because it is not possible to assess the number of moral damages and determine the equivalent of such damages. On the other hand, due to the prevalence of some areas of moral damage objection and the specific complexities of the issue, the judicial courts are less involved in these complications and there will be less opportunity to deal with the specific subtleties of this issue.

In any case, there are common ways to compensate spiritual losses, which are briefly mentioned below

- ✓ Stopping or eliminating the source of damage.
- ✓ Verbal apology for the damage.
- ✓ Practical or written apology or inclusion of apologies in newspapers.
- ✓ Restoring dignity from damage suffered in any other way.
- ✓ Payment of material property to the damaged.

The first case of compensation for the above-mentioned damages is actually the same subject concerned with article 8 of the civil liability law, and it follows from the text of the article that the legislator's concern in issuing the said article is the reputation and commercial and professional reputation of the individual and seeks to compensate for that damage.

In this case, it will include limited cases of moral compensation. The second and third cases of the common ways of compensation for spiritual damages are only used in small and minor spiritual damages and are effective, otherwise, large damages such as reputational, honor and emotional damages, hurting people's emotions, putting pressure mental and psychological damage cannot be compensated by apologizing or publishing an announcement in the newspaper or the like. The fourth way of compensation for spiritual damage is also used according to article 171 of the constitution and it is an example of the other cases mentioned above, and nothing else comes to mind to confirm it.

This is the reason why it can be said: The most effective way to compensate the moral damages of the fifth case is to pay the property of the victim. Other punishments and criminal enforcement guarantees are for the purpose of maintaining social order and respecting the rights of society, if personal damages are caused to the injured person.

Therefore, it must be said: no means will be more effective than paying money or transferring money, and of course, to do this, the necessary proportion must be established between the mental pressures involved.

Chapter V

Conclusion

An intellectual work can be interpreted as wealth if it has wealth or a useful element and also has a rarity element. Of course, the requirement of the legislator to fulfill the conditions of intellectual work, having originality and the existence of innovation for the creator has been listed. These two conditions make the intellectual work have two exclusive rights, material and spiritual, and in addition to property, it envisages ownership for it. Property can be divided into two types of material property such as houses and cars and intellectual property such as scientific, literary or artistic works. The utility and usefulness of intellectual works are generally agreed, although there may be intellectual works that are not only not useful but also have disadvantages. So, this type of intellectual works may not be considered as property in a society if they are not useful, like stray books in Islamic societies, but due to rarity and right of appropriation, it can be property, but the condition of rarity is also for intellectual works under the condition of originality and the researcher's initiative. Undoubtedly, an intellectual work is considered property and a distinction should be made between the intellectual work and the carrier of the intellectual work. Protectable intellectual work is the original work itself, not the book or magazine or device that is invented.

For example, Hafez's poetry and the book of Hafez's poetry collection are two separate categories. The intellectual work is the essence and essence of Hafez's poetry, which is of course rare. The book of Hafez's poems is the carrier of Hafez's intellectual works, and its publication does not damage the rarity of Hafez's works. In the matter of invention, it is actually the intellectual work of the invented idea and formula, not a device that indicates the function of the invented formula. That formula is considered a property due to scarcity and can be supported.

The result is that the intellectual work is financial, which has exclusive material and spiritual rights, and this property, in addition to being beneficial, is also desirable intellectually, and of course, according to the condition of originality and innovation, it also has an element of rarity, but in contrast to this opinion of the elders and jurists. There are those who either disagree with the origin of the property, or with the author's ownership of the work, or with the monopoly in publishing it. Imam Khomeini is the leader of the contemporary jurists who opposed the monopoly in the publication of the work, and while accepting the creator's right of ownership requires the exercise of the owner's right of appropriation, and this right cannot be applied only to the work, but also extends to the scope of the work's bearer. The owner's dominion limits the work.

The authority of the owner of the work is valid as long as it does not threaten the authority of the owner of the work. The last word is that an intellectual work, including scientific, literary, artistic, invention, and the like, is considered property, and although its objectivity is not tangible in the material world, its external appearance has meaning in the world and can be touched mentally, in such a way that external and known effects the greatest and most valuable assets today are intellectual assets, with which one can do things that were impossible in the past. For example, a software that does not have a tangible material existence in the physical world, allows you to send and guide spaceships and discoveries in other worlds, or today there is a software called windows that is produced and sold by the richest person in the world. has constructed.

Now that this work is considered property, several rights can be proven on it, including: material rights, intellectual rights and other rights such as the right of appropriation, the right of benefit and finally the right of ownership. In fact, the intellectual property right of the works is known as the right to control the copying of the work and control its other uses for a certain period of time in different legal systems and at the level of the international legal system.

Today, with the emergence and expansion of digital media, especially the expansion of computer networks and the Internet, new possibilities have been provided both to control and express these works and to escape from this control. In the meantime, the owners of the work are encouraged to maintain their work and people are also encouraged to have free and wide access, but there is also a new challenge that this work is a product and income or has been evaluated as a public good, of course, governments through the contracts and international agreements have always sought to protect these rights, regardless of the fact that sometimes the complexity and contradictions in the world of communication are beyond the jurisdiction of governments. With this introduction, the subject of intellectual property in Iranian criminal law has been entered, and it can be said that both in the Sharia law and in the current laws of the Islamic Republic of Iran, the possibility of moral damages is recognized, and the affected person can, in addition to material damages, damages also demand the spiritual that has been brought in.

Therefore, in the current practice, moral damages can be claimed according to the civil liability law and the criminal procedure law, although according to the general court procedure law and the revolution approved in 1378, it is not possible to claim moral damage contrary to the procedural law of 1290. In the new criminal procedure law, this issue has been resolved and the right to claim moral damages has been clarified. Also, in a separate note, the legislator has mentioned the definition of moral damages. Beyond the possibility of claiming moral damages, the possibility of calendaring moral damages is questioned.

Because moral damages are not objective and tangible financial losses, but the said damages are in fact the damage to the professional reputation, social dignity, and reputation of individuals. This damage certainly cannot be measured with money. Therefore, in some courts, they refrain from issuing judicial rulings to compensate for this category of damages, and sometimes silence is adopted. So far, we have found that apart from the difficulty of claiming moral damages, there is also the difficulty of calculating moral damages to property, but we know that in the Civil Liability Law and in article 10 of it, a series of examples are mentioned for compensation of moral damages, all of which It is spiritual and non-financial. For example, in the same article, it is required to apologize and enter the judgment in the newspaper, among other spiritual examples, in order to relieve and calm the victim and in some way to compensate for the spiritual losses.

Of course, the new bill of the criminal procedure for compensation for mental injuries or damage to personal or family dignity and reputation is limited to restoration of dignity, restoration of reputation or determining the amount of costs for removing mental injuries after obtaining an expert opinion. In this way, it can be said: the legislator has tried to compensate the moral damage in both non-material and material ways, but this doubt and important issue remains that in reality, how and with what method and criteria should this restoration of dignity and prestige be done take.

Therefore, it can be concluded that despite the legal capacity to follow up and claim moral damages according to the explicit texts of the law, the issuance of a judgment for the payment of moral damages in the stage of determining the amount of damages caused to the victim due to the lack of criteria and indicators that can be measured and addressed, as well as the lack of It will be difficult to convince the judge's conscience to issue a definitive and binding sentence. For example, in each specific case, we must find out what the victim's mind was calmed by in relation to each specific issue, in order to restore his dignity in the same way, but the possibility of issuing a general verdict in this regard is ruled out and will not be possible.

Violation of intellectual rights can be divided into several categories in terms of profit and loss for the infringer and the right holder

- ✓ The infringer will benefit from the act of violation and at the same time the owner of the right will be harmed.
- ✓ The infringer benefits from the act of infringement, but the owner of the right is not harmed.
- ✓ The infringer does not benefit from the act of violation and the owner of the right is harmed.
- ✓ The infringer does not benefit from the act of violation and the owner of the right does not suffer any loss.
- ✓ The infringer did not benefit from the act of infringement and the right holder benefited from it in some way.

It is obvious that wherever a loss has occurred to the owner of the right, he can demand compensation for his loss by referring to the relevant provisions, including the civil liability law and the specific provisions of intellectual property rights. In this case, it does not make a difference whether the violator has also benefited from the violation of the right or not? But where the damage to the intellectual property owner is not certain, such as the assumption that the inventor simply registered his invention without commercializing it.

If, in these cases, the infringer benefits and at the same time the property of the right holder is reduced, and the causal relationship between this increase and decrease is proven, there is no doubt that a verdict can be given to restore the benefits obtained against the infringer, but it seems that there are several problems here. First, as it was said, intellectual rights have a special nature and their use without permission does not necessarily mean a reduction of property, especially in the case of the discussed assumption that the owner of the invention has only taken the initiative to register it in the offices of the Patent Office. Secondly, in some cases, the violation of the right may not only cause loss to the owner, but also may not result in profit for the violator.

For example, in this case, if the infringer produces products after using another invention to market, but before entering the market, all the products are destroyed due to a fire in the storage warehouse, despite the violation of the patent, the infringer's profit accrues has not been therefore, the owner of the right cannot benefit from the guarantee of patent infringement executions provided in the patent law. Because according to article 181 of the executive regulations of the patent law, in the case of damages that are claimed either through legal channels or through criminal channels in lawsuits related to patents, industrial designs, trademarks and trade names, the damages will include the losses incurred.

Therefore, it can be said that applying the rule of unjust possession to compensate the intellectual rights owners is not possible and will not necessarily lead to compensation from them.

References

Aslani, Hamid Reza, Industrial property rights in cyberspace, 2010, first edition, Tehran, Mizan Publishing.

Amir Saed, lawyer, protection of intellectual property in the World Trade Organization and Iran Law, 2004, first edition, Tehran, Majd Publications.

Emami, Seyyed Hassan, 1987, Civil Rights, Tehran, Islamic Bookstore Publications, Ch6, Vol.1.

Emami Asadullah, 2016, Industrial Property Rights, Tehran, Mizan Publishing.

Ansari, Baqir, Laws of Mass Communication, 2017, second edition, Tehran, Samt Publications.

Aiti, Hamid, 1996, Rights of Intellectual Creations, Tehran, Laws of Law, Ch.1.

Babaei, Iraj, 2015, the place of separation of loss and compensation in civil liability, legal research, vol. 76.

Jafarzadeh, Ali, 2011, requirements without contract and forced guarantee, Tehran, Jangal Publishing.

Jafarzadeh, Mirqasem, Ghazizadeh, Mohammad Reza, 2012, Civil liability for patent infringement, fault-based or absolute liability? Journal of legal research, special issue No. 13.

Jafarzadeh, Mir Qasim, an introduction to the rights of intellectual creations, textbook, first semester of the academic year 2014-2015, Shahid Beheshti University.

Jafari Tabar, Hassan, 2013, spiritual property in the side; In the philosophy of intellectual property rights, Tehran, publishing company, Ch. 1.

Jafari Langroudi, Mohammad Jaafar, 1993, Legal Terminology, Tehran, Ganj Danesh.

Hojjati Ashrafi, Gholamreza, complete set of laws and regulations of trade and commerce, 2004, first edition, Tehran, Ganj Danesh.

Hikmatnia, Mahmoud, 2018, jurisprudential and economic review of intellectual property, Islamic Economy, ninth year, no. 33.

Hekmatnia, Mahmoud, Fundamentals of Intellectual Property, 2007, 1st edition, Tehran, Islamic Culture and Thought Research Institute Publishing Organization.

Khomeini, Ruhollah, 2009, Kitab al-Bai, Tehran, Imam Khomeini Editing and Publishing Institute, vol.1.

Dehkhoda, Ali Akbar, 2010, Dehkhoda dictionary, Tehran, Tehran University Press, vol.1.

Rajabi, Abdullah, 2016, civil guarantee due to violation of intellectual right: liability lawsuit or estifa? Islamic law, year 14, no. 55.

Rajabi, Abdullah, Abbasi Wafaei, Mehdi, 2015, Law Governing the Violation of Intellectual Rights, Specialized Quarterly of Religion and Law, No. 12.

Rahmani, Mohammad, 1997, Rules of jurisprudence: the rule of waste, Ahl al-Bayt Fiqh Magazine, Nos. 11 and 12.

Zahedi, Mehdi, 2000, Laws of trademark registration: a comparative study in the laws of Iran and the World Trade Organization, Law and Politics Research Journal, first year, second issue, spring and summer.

Zarkalam, Sattar, 2013, Literary and Artistic Property Rights, Tehran, Samt.

Zarkalam, Sattar, Literary and news property rights, 2009, Tehran, Smit.

Sheikhi, Maryam, guaranteeing the enforcement of literary and artistic property rights in Iran and international agreements, Judicial Law Journal, numbers 50 and 51.

Sadeghi, Mohsen, 2008, supporting pharmaceutical innovations and joining the World Trade Organization, Tehran, Mizan Publishing, Ch1.

Sadeghi, Hossein, 2009, civil responsibility in electronic communications, first edition, Tehran, Mizan Publishing.

Sadeghi, Toubi, 2014, competition law in the field of intellectual property, Master's thesis, Shahid Beheshti University, Faculty of Law.

Safai, Seyyed Hossein, 2012, Civil Laws and Comparative Laws, Tehran, Mizan.

Safai, Seyyed Hossein, Rahimi, Habibullah, 2013, Civil liability (obligations outside the contract), Tehran, position.

Alidoust, Abolqasem, 2015, unjust and unjust acquisition in Iran's legal system, a new exploration in jurisprudence, year 33, no. 1.

Omid, Hassan, 1990, Farhang Omid, Tehran, Amirkabir Publications, Ch3.

Omid Zanjani, Abbas Ali, 2003, "Majibat Daman", an introduction to civil liability and its causes and effects in Islamic jurisprudence, Tehran, Mizan Publishing House, ch.1.

Issai Tafarshi, Mohammad, Sadeghi, Mahmoud, Shahmohammadi, Mohammad, 2013, investigation of exemplary remuneration as a compensation rule for patent infringement and comparative study with conventional royalties in American law, Judicial Law Journal, Vol. 78.

Isai Tafarshi, Mohammad; Sadeghi, Mahmoud, Shah Mohammadi, Mohammad, 2013, Diversion of the owner's benefit, a rule for compensating damages caused by patent infringement in Iranian and American law, Comparative Law Research, Volume 15, Issue 3.

Microsoft Internet and Network Dictionary, 2013, translated by Masoud Pak Nazar, first edition, Ganj Shaygan.

Ghasemi, Mohsen, 2006, the evolution of author's rights in the international community, legal magazine of the International Law Service Office of the Islamic Republic of Iran, number 35.

Qanad, Fatemeh, 2018, Rights arising from secrets and trademarks in cyberspace, Criminal science updates, collection of articles, Tehran, Mizan Legal Foundation.

Katouzian, Nasser, 1995, Obligations outside the contract: Forced guarantee, Tehran, University of Tehran Publishing and Printing Institute, Ch3, Vol.1 and 2.

Kazemi, Mahmoud, Pilwar, Rahim, 2017, genealogy of property, a comparative study in Islamic and Western law, Islamic Law Research Journal, year 19, no. 47.

Lotfi, Asadullah, 2001, Rules of civil jurisprudence, Tehran, Samt, vol.1.

Mohagheq Damad, Seyyed Mostafi, 2009, Jurisprudence Rules 1, Civil Department, Tehran, Islamic Publishing Center, Ch19.

Mohammadi, Pejman, Muradpourshad, Amir, Mobin, Hojjat, 2017, the effect of the Criminal Procedure Law approved in 2012 on the possibility of claiming moral damages and loss of profit in Iran's legal system, private legal research, volume 7, no. 24.

Madani, Mahsa, Farrokhi, Zohra, 2017, comparative study of trademark infringement elements in American and Iranian law, private law research, no. 24.

Mousavi, Seyed Mohammad Sadegh, Khazaei, Seyed Ali, Dehghan, Seyed Hadi, 2017, comparative study of economic damage and lack of benefit, comparative research of Islamic and Western law, volume 5, no. 2.

Mir Hosseini, Seyyed Hassan, Culture of intellectual property rights, 2015, second volume, literary and artistic property rights, first edition.

Mir Hosseini, Seyyed Hasan, 2015, Laws of Industrial Designs, Tehran, Mizan Legal Foundation.

Mirhosseini, Seyyed Hassan, 2017, Introduction to intellectual property rights, second edition, Tehran, Mizan Publishing.

Wasali, Mahmoud Reza, 2000, analysis of regulations related to trade marks in Iranian and comparative laws, PhD thesis, Azad University, Research Sciences Unit.

Hedayati Mehboob, Abolfazl, Asadi, Mohammad Hassan, 2018, a critique on Article 14 of the Criminal Procedure Law, Private Law Research, Volume 7, No. 26.

Printed by Books on Demand GmbH, Norderstedt / Germany